FREDERICK LEONG, PH.D.
THE OHIO STATE UNIVERSITY
DEPARTMENT OF PSYCHOLOGY
142 TOWNSHEND HALL
1885 NEIL AVENUE MALL
COLUMBUS OHIO 43210-1222

D1030214

Time and Human Interaction

TIME AND
HUMAN INTERACTION

Toward a Social Psychology of Time

JOSEPH E. MCGRATH
JANICE R. KELLY
University of Illinois, Urbana

The Guilford Press
New York   London

© 1986 The Guilford Press
A Division of Guilford Publications, Inc.
200 Park Avenue South, New York, N.Y. 10003

Printed in the United States of America

Library of Congress Cataloging in Publication Data

McGrath, Joseph Edward, 1927–
    Time and human interaction.

    (The Guilford social psychology series)
    Bibliography: p.
    Includes index.
    1. Social interaction.   2. Time—Social aspects.
3. Time—Psychological aspects.   I. Kelly, Janice R.
II. Title.   III. Series.
HM291.M3945   1986   302   86-396
ISBN 0–89862–111–9

P R E F A C E

To study time is a scholar's delight! The development of this book has been driven by the sheer fun of it.

After all, we have been privileged to spend our "work" time exploring intriguing ideas in philosophy and natural science; reviewing interesting portions of the psychological literature; designing, conducting, and interpreting challenging experiments; and exploring a series of fascinating methodological issues. What more could two dedicated academics wish for!

But to make things even better, besides being fun, the study of time at the social-psychological level is important. It is a relatively uncharted area, with new ideas awaiting researchers at every turn. It is a topical area too long neglected. And, we believe, it will be even more important in the future. We are thrice privileged.

We have had help and support from a number of people. The overall research program on which the book is based has had some direct and indirect support from the Psychology Department, the Center for Advanced Study, and the University Research Board, all of the University of Illinois, Urbana. Nancy Rotchford, Diane Machatka, and Susan Murphy were collaborators on parts of the research program.

Irwin Altman, Robert Baron, and J. Richard Hackman were generous in both their encouragement and their constructive criticism on the penultimate draft of this material. Many colleagues gave us assistance and helpful reviews on earlier drafts of parts of this material, among them: James Davis, Kimberly

Carter-Hays, Stuart Oskamp, Daniel Stokols, Rebecca Warner, Carol Werner, and Allen Wicker.

Some of the ideas presented in this book are based on material we have already published, in more detailed form, in journal articles and chapters of other books. We appreciate the helpful advice of several anonymous reviewers of those manuscripts.

Finally, we are grateful for having had the opportunity to do some of the work on this material while serving as "summer fellows" at the Baldwin Research Institute and the Beaver Island Educational Center, respectively. We are privileged, indeed!

Joseph E. McGrath
Janice R. Kelly

C O N T E N T S

C H A P T E R 1

Introduction

TIME AND SOCIAL PSYCHOLOGY

*For what is time? Who is able easily and briefly to explain that?
Who is able . . . to comprehend it, so as to express himself concerning
it? And yet what in our usual discourse do we more familiarly and
knowingly make mention of than time? And surely, we understand
it well enough when we speak of it; we understand it also when in
speaking with another we hear it named. What is time then? If
nobody asks me, I know, but if I were desirous to explain it to one
that should ask me, plainly I know not.*
— St. Augustine's Confessions, Book 11, Chapter 14.

Time is a part of the fabric of our lives. The ordinary business
of human social behavior teems with temporal considerations.
Time concepts and expressions permeate our language and
thought. And yet, social psychology, a field that purports to
study human social behavior, is relatively "timeless." How can
we as social psychologists ignore a dimension that is so central
to human life?

That time is important in human affairs seems hardly to
need documentation. In our culture, time is sometimes regarded as a scarce and therefore valuable resource, to be "saved"
or at least not "wasted." We often see our problems as resulting from not having enough time; occasionally we see them
as resulting from having too much time on our hands. We face
deadlines and time limits; so time becomes a source (or jus-
tification) of much of our anxiety. We all wish for that extra
hour in the day, that extra day in the week, to finish all that

we have to do. We have to pack a lot of living into our limited ration of time.

Time is also a major source of hope, and of fear. We will know in due time; time heals all wounds; who knows what time will bring. Time is the carriage for the great unfolding of events, some of which we anticipate with joy and some of which we dread.

But what is time? The quote from Augustine at the start of this chapter reflects time's dual aspects, the obvious and the unknown. Time can be thought of in many ways. One is to view it as an external process that regulates our lives. In that view, time is a clock that ticks away seconds, minutes, and hours. Time is that measure by which we know when to get up, when to go to work, when to eat, when to sleep. Time is a calendar that differentiates one day from another—workdays and weekends, holidays and birthdays. Time moves inexorably, and we must always try to keep up with it.

Sometimes we think of time as a more personal, internal process. Our experience of two equal periods of clock time can differ dramatically. Sometimes we get so caught up in events that time passes too quickly. Other times, when we are bored, time passes too slowly. One minute does not necessarily feel just like every other minute. Such internal time is an integral part of our experience of events.

Time and the Study of Social Psychology

Time has been given much attention in many scientific and intellectual disciplines. Questions about the nature of time have been of concern to philosophers for centuries. Time has been a focus of considerable attention in physics and biology; and temporal matters have received some attention in anthropology and experimental psychology as well. But social psychology has given virtually no attention to time in its theory or research. For the most part, it has failed to study temporal features of social behavior in much the same way that, until quite recently, it failed to study space and place and other aspects of the physical environment.

For instance, there has been very little research on the effects of time pressure at either the group or individual level, even though time pressure is known to be one of the major sources of stress and anxiety. There also has been very little social psychological research on the effects of various temporal orientations, past, present, and future, although there has been some cross-cultural research on this topic.

Temporal factors are ubiquitous in our methodology as well, but we seldom recognize their significance. For instance, we often use delays, latencies, and rate and duration measures; but these are almost always considered as ways to measure or control other variables, not as parameters interesting in their own right. Virtually every experiment is temporally bounded— by the experimental hour or some other brief data-collection period. Yet the assumptions and limitations involved in this time boundedness are seldom noted. Many of the threats to valid causal conclusions are temporal in nature (e.g., history, maturation, attrition). Indeed, a known temporal order is essential to draw a causal inference at all. And, while we know that we must carefully control intervals between treatments and observations so that alternative hypotheses will not cloud our interpretations, we seldom deal with such time intervals as an integral part of the interpretation of the causal process itself.

The current paradigms of our field mask the importance of time in several ways that make it more difficult and less rewarding to study temporal matters. In part, we have defined time away by asserting that time is not a "real" variable but "merely" a medium within which objects exist and events take place. It is not time itself that is important, goes this argument, but rather the events and experience that "fill" time.

Futhermore, our current methodological paradigms emphasize research strategies that dissociate the relations to be examined from the context—temporal or otherwise—within which those relations take place. Those "context stripping" strategies not only "control" temporal factors so that they do not confound results; they also serve to insulate the researcher from "discovering" major temporal relations in the phenomena under study. In laboratory experiments, we look at behavior during very small periods of time in artificial contexts. Our paradigm forces such high control and artificiality as part of the price we pay to be able to make definitive causal statements about the phenomena under study. In field research, we often do little better with respect to time; we study the phenomena of concern in contexts that are "natural," but nonetheless static.

Other reasons for our general failure to study time in social psychology are pragmatic. It takes time to study time; and it costs a lot in other resources too. Some earlier efforts in social psychology had an inherently temporal character: for example, Bales's (1950) pioneering work on phase and cycles in inter-action process; early studies of delayed effects in attitude change and social influence; studies of group development, sociali-zation, and the like. These research efforts never really cap-tured center stage in social psychology, and work on them soon declined, in part because of their high costs and in part because we did not (then) have the sophisticated methodolog-ical and statistical tools necessary to examine the temporal character of those phenomena.

In the conceptual arena, social psychology has given lots of lip service, but precious little intellectual effort, to such time-based concepts as "process," "dynamics," and "change." In social psychology, the word *dynamics* has become largely a popular rubric, shorn of all those temporal qualities that it carries when used in the physical sciences (thermodynamics really does study processes over time!). We too often have studied "process" (when we have studied it at all) by making inferences from differences between two system states sepa-rated by some arbitrary amount of time. This "difference be-tween time-ordered states" is not irrelevant to the study of social processes; but it is by no means the method of choice for studying them, especially for those processes that might be nonlinear or nonmonotonic. That approach is like trying to understand an ongoing behavior sequence by examining two time-ordered (but otherwise arbitrarily selected) frames from a film of that action.

Above all, though, social psychology has failed to study temporal factors because we have worked almost exclusively from a paradigm that presumes a central role for equilibrium–adaptation processes. In that model, *change is regarded as transitory.* It is either epiphenomenal error variance; or it is an undesirable perturbation of an inherently stable system. Both of these potential sources of change lose their importance as a result of theories that postulate equilibrium-seeking, or dissonance-reducing, or balance-restoring processes, and of data-analysis operations that eliminate unwanted variability by averaging away the variance over time. That, too, reflects a non-thoughtful acceptance of the culture's dominant conception of time (and causality, and change, and the nature of things) that contains ideas that trace back through Newton, Descartes, and Aristotle to Democritus. Alternatively, we could (and Heraclitus did) take the view that *change and process* are real, as figure against the background of momentarily balanced epiphenomenal "system states." In current social psychology, Altman and colleagues (e.g., Altman, Vinsel, & Brown, 1981) take such a Heraclitean view that carries with it an impetus to study process and change and the temporal aspects underlying them. But few social psychologists have followed that path; most have accepted without concern both the equilibrium–adaptation model and its accompanying de-emphasis of the importance of change. With that view has also come a downplaying of the importance of temporal processes.

In any case, as a result of these and probably other features of our paradigms and practices, we now have an almost completely "timeless" social psychology—in the worst literal meaning, not the more positive metaphorical meaning, of that phrase.

Some social psychologists have begun to study these matters, however, even though most have not. For example, we can find temporal constructs deeply embedded within Thibaut and Kelley's exchange theory (Kelley & Thibaut, 1978; Thibaut & Kelley, 1959); within Altman's work on social penetration (Altman & Taylor, 1973), privacy (Altman, 1975), and the dialectics of interpersonal interaction (Altman et al., 1981); and within the work of Kahn and colleagues on stress in organizations (Kahn, Wolfe, Quinn, Snoek, & Rosenthal, 1964; Katz & Kahn, 1976).

Thibaut and Kelley, for example, talk about development of norms in dyadic exchange relations in terms of simultaneity, alternation, sequencing, and various other complex orderings of behavior of persons A and B in relation to each other. Altman and Taylor's treatment of the social penetration process is an explicitly time-based conceptual schema. Altman's work on privacy treats the control of the flow of interpersonal interaction as an explicitly dynamic process in which changes in desired levels (of interaction given and received), as well as changes in environmental events and conditions, provide a continuous, dynamic, bidirectional multivariate pattern of interaction over time. Furthermore, in the Altman work and in the Thibaut and Kelley work as well, other time-based concepts such as "satiation, "adaptation," and "anticipation" are crucial.

Temporal factors also loom large in the work of Kahn and colleagues on role stress. Many aspects of role stress are played out in time—and so are many features of the behavior involved in coping with them. People compartmentalize their time to reduce at least some role conflicts, and to manage or try to manage role overloads.

All three of these bodies of work—exchange theory, social penetration and privacy, and role conflict—offer the beginnings of a body of research and theory that takes time into account. But they only begin to touch on the many temporal features that are a part of human social behavior. Indeed, there is an astonishing array of temporal features involved even within a single topic. Take, for example, the study of social-psychological aspects of stress. Some of the temporally tinged factors that are important features in that topical area include:

- the *anticipation interval* before the stressor;
- the *duration* of the stressor;
- the *duration* of the situation within which the stressor occurs;
- *maturation* of the person in the situation;

- the *prior experience* of the person with the situation;
- *time needed* for the operation of coping mechanisms;
- temporal features of the coping mechanisms themselves (e.g., *preventive* coping, *anticipatory* coping, *reactive* coping, *delayed* coping); and
- temporal aspects of such concepts as *"adaptation," "adjustment," "fatigue"* and *"learning."*

Even this partial list of temporal factors in stress and coping illustrates that, whether or not the researcher wishes to deal with them, temporal considerations pervade most of the complex research problems of social psychology.

We can distinguish temporal features of social behavior along a continuum from more micro to more macro levels of time. The very intricate patterns of synchronization and sequencing that characterize ongoing interpersonal interaction are at a moderately micro level of time (from about 3- to about 20-minute periods). There is extensive research, for example, on interruptions, silences, simultaneous speech, turn taking, and the like, within verbal communication; and related research on various coordinated features of nonverbal communication (cf. Argyle & Dean, 1965; Dabbs, 1983; Gottman, 1979). These involve complex temporal patternings of multiple sets of responses by multiple social actors. These patterns have been expressed by such terms as "mutuality," "reciprocity," "complementarity," "dominance," "similarity," "simultaneity," and "alternation."

At a more macro level of time, we can look at such things as the temporal ordering and sequencing of events within an organization. For a smooth flow of an organization's activities, there must be an ordering and synchronization of different organizational functions: product development, testing, production, marketing, and the like. You cannot test what you have not yet developed; nor should you produce what is not yet tested. But this is more than a simple order or chain of activities. You can market what is still being produced, and indeed, smooth long-run functioning requires such overlap between and coordination among activities.

At even more macro levels of time, we can look at such things as stages in the life course, or cyclical recurrences of fashion over generations. The point, here, is that temporal features abound at every level of social behavior to which we might want to apply our conceptual and methodological tools.

So, we believe, temporal matters are pervasive, important, and, until now, largely neglected within social psychology. Therefore, we argue, we need to develop a social psychology of time. That is, we need to mount a systematic effort to identify, study, and try to understand the many temporal features that are inherent within the conceptual, substantive, and methodological material of social psychology. This book represents our attempt to begin such a venture.

The Organization and Contents of This Book

Temporal issues can enter into social-psychological research in any of three capacities, or "functional roles."

1. Temporal factors can serve as "independent variables," so to speak, in social-psychological research. That is, we can study how various temporal factors may affect various aspects of the social behavior of individuals, singly or in group or organizational settings. This functional role for time implies questions like: "How do (various temporal features of personal, situational, and environmental variables) affect (various aspects of individual, group, or organizational behavior)? For instance, how does time pressure affect individual problem-solving performance?

2. Temporal factors can be a source of methodological problems for social-psychological studies of any content area. That is, we can study how various temporal factors may influence our research strategy, designs, measures, and manipulations in studies of *any* social-psychological content. This functional role implies questions like: "How is the relation between (various social psychological factors serving as "independent variables") and (various aspects of individual, group, or organizational behavior serving as "dependent variables")

affected by (various temporal features of the study strategy, design, and operations)? For instance, how does the length of time between an experimental treatment and the measurement of its effects influence the magnitude and the form of that relation?

3. Temporal factors can serve as "dependent variables" in social-psychological research. That is, we can study how various social and psychological factors may affect the way humans conceptualize, experience, and use time, and how those factors may alter the temporal patterning of behavior. This functional role implies questions like: How do (various individual, situational, and environmental factors, serving as "independent variables") affect (various features of human experience and use of time, and various features of the temporal patterns underlying human behavior)? For instance, how do the mood states of two interacting individuals affect the temporal patterning of their conversational behavior?

In this book, we deal to some degree with work on all three of those functional roles. Work on time pressure (see Chapter 4) and on the effects of work shifts (see Chapter 5) deal with time as independent variable. Many issues raised about the temporal characteristics of measures and about the temporal course of causal processes (Chapter 6) deal with time as the source of methodological problems. The evidence regarding social entrainment of task performance and interaction (Chapter 4), and the material on judging the experience of time (Chapter 3), as well as material on conflicting conceptions of time (Chapters 2 and 3), deal with time as dependent variable. A full-fledged social psychology of time needs to incorporate time in all three of these capacities.

We can consider the material in the main chapters of this book as dealing with the impact of temporal factors in conceptual, substantive, and methodological aspects of our field. Chapter 2 and 3 deal, primarily, with conceptual matters. Chapters 4 and 5 deal mainly with substantive material. Chapter 6 deals with methodological considerations. We will now preview the main ideas offered in that material in that same order of presentation.

Chapter 2 addresses the question: "What is the nature of time?" In that chapter, we explore some of the different ways in which time can be conceptualized. We start by examining some of the major issues in the philosophy of time. For instance: Is time homogeneous or differentiated? Is it abstract or concrete? Is time reversible or irreversible? And is there but one correct time, or can there be multiple time constructs, each valid for its own domain?

None of those questions have a correct answer. Rather, each culture (and subculture) has a preferred position(s) on each of the questions. Those preferred positions, together, make up that culture's dominant conception of time. In any given case, there are likely to be major subcultural variants of that conception, as well.

The dominant conception of time in Western culture has been heavily influenced by classical Newtonian physics. Here, for instance, time is considered as abstract, divisible, homogeneous, and as a singular, independent dimension. Other variant conceptions are emerging, but their impact on the lay culture is as yet very slight. These variant conceptions include aspects of thought emerging from the "new physics" (Einsteinian physics), from biology (which draws heavily on notions of cycles), and from the philosophies of Eastern mysticism. In Chapter 2, we discuss these temporal issues in relation to those dominant and variant conceptions of time in our culture.

CHAPTER 3: TIME AND HUMAN EXPERIENCE

Chapter 3 addresses questions about time at the individual level. We live our lives amidst a myriad of time frames, some of which are tied to the culturally dominant and variant conceptions of time and some of which exist on a more personal level. For instance, we can "locate" ourselves, at any given time in relation to the secular calendar that is accepted in our culture; in terms of the number of birthdays we personally have had; in terms of our position in a career cycle; and/or in terms of our position in a family life cycle.

How can we bring harmony among those various time frames, or otherwise deal with their differences? This is not an easy thing to resolve, especially when some of those time frames are based on conceptions of time that are in direct conflict with each other. Think, for example, about a person to whom job seniority means enhanced value due to experience, who works in a company for which seniority means reduced value due to obsolescence.

In Chapter 3, we describe some of these time frames and discuss some of the conflicts that can occur among them. We also discuss how some of those varying time frames and conceptions affect the individual. For instance, what are the implications of treating time as a scarce resource as opposed to treating it as a relatively abundant "free good"?

We end Chapter 3 with a new look at an old problem— psychophysical judgments of the duration of time intervals. Traditionally, investigators have looked at this problem as an effort to assess accuracy of perceptions of time judged against an objectively correct standard of outside clock time. An alternative way to view such time judgments would treat them as the juxtaposition of two time frames or conceptions, neither of which is to be regarded as a standard for the other.

CHAPTER 4: THE RHYTHMS OF SOCIAL BEHAVIOR

Why do people experience jet lag? In our everday lives, many of our physiological and social processes become coupled together (mutually entrained) and are in synchrony with the diurnal cycle of the planet (externally entrained). When we travel rapidly through different time zones, these processes become uncoupled from outside time, and become uncoupled from each other because they re-adapt to outside time at different rates. That desynchronization of physiological and social rhythms is what people experience as jet lag. Eventually, these processes will become entrained again and the jet lag effects will disappear.

The concept of entrainment is of long standing in the biological sciences. In fact, some biologists have argued that entrainment is the fundamental principle of organization within biological systems. But entrainment can also occur in social processes. Such social entrainment is the topic of Chapter 4.

We propose a model of social entrainment and describe how social processes, such as task-performance rate and quality, the flow of conversations, the patterning of nonverbal behavior, and the like, can become coupled together—that is, entrained. This can occur as mutual entrainment of various processes within a single individual, or as mutual entrainment of sets of processes between two or more people who are in interaction with one another. For example, conversation flow for two interacting people often can become mutually entrained at two quite different levels: In the short run (a matter of seconds, minutes), their periods of speech and silences tend to become complementary (180 degrees out of phase); whereas over a longer period (a matter of hours, or segments of a day), their periods of high vocal activity and periods of low vocal activity tend to occur at the same time (i.e., in phase). Furthermore, such social processes can become entrained to certain external cycles or signals—just as the processes underlying jet lag become entrained to the planet's day–night cycle. In Chapter 4, we discuss how some past research findings—our own and those of other researchers—can easily be interpreted within the proposed social entrainment model.

CHAPTER 5: TIME AND WORK

Most work organizations carry the dominant cultural conception of time (as scarce, linear, divisible, homogeneous, and so forth) as part of their underlying philosophy. This gives rise to certain key problems, temporal in character, for both the organization and its members. Three key temporal problems for organizations that are partly consequences of the culturally dominant conception of time are: temporal ambiguity, temporally conflicting demands, and the inherent scarcity of time.

The responses of organizations to these problems involve the temporal processes of scheduling, synchronization, and allocation. These, in turn, give rise to some associated temporal problems for the individual, namely the temporal aspects of role ambiguity, role conflict, and role overload. An analysis of these matters provides a kind of macrostructure, or context, for understanding the operation of endogenous rhythms in work organizations, and of their entrainment to one another and to outside "pacers."

The entrainment model also provides a unifying fabric for discussing a number of studies done on temporal aspects of behavior in organizations. Notable among these are studies of how working "nonnormal" shifts can affect the worker's productivity, safety, sleep patterns, and other aspects of physical and psychological health, job satisfaction, and relations with family and friends. The complex implications of the findings of these studies can be clarified a lot, we believe, by use of the entrainment model. We can regard the off-time work schedule as a major external entrainment force that desynchronizes a whole panoply of temporal patterns, not only within that individual but between the worker and his or her social networks in and outside of the workplace. Furthermore, we can regard the individual's condition and behavior as efforts to adapt to, resynchronize with, or otherwise cope with, those (dis)entrainment effects.

CHAPTER 6: TIME AND THE LOGIC OF METHOD

Time is ubiquitous in the methodology of our field. There are temporal features of many of our measures and manipulations; and there are temporal considerations that are fundamental to the logic of our methods as well.

For instance, in order to draw valid causal conclusions, we all know that the effect cannot precede the cause in time. There must be a known temporal ordering of cause and effect. Furthermore, temporal considerations permeate our research strategies and designs. For instance, most of the threats to internal validity of studies are temporal in nature (e.g., history, maturation, attrition, etc.).

With time so prevalent in our methods, it is surprising that the treatment of time in our methodology has been so cavalier. For instance, we often base decisions about how long to let study participants perform a task on quite atheoretical, arbitrary grounds: either on what other researchers have done in previous studies, or on constraints of the experimental hour. Furthermore, we often make strong assumptions about how time measures map to the underlying processes based on a fairly casual acceptance of the culture's dominant conception of time. For example, we often assume that processes unfold in time in a monotonic, linear fashion, and therefore that "longer" means "more." But many biological, psychological, and social processes operate in a cyclical fashion, thus confounding the logic of our time measure.

Perhaps the most damaging temporal problem of all is the lack of fit between our methods and our theories in regard to the temporal intervals necessary for causal processes to unfold. Often, we impose an experimental treatment, and at a specific later time we measure the effects. Very rarely do we work from a theory that is so carefully defined as to specify *how long* that interval should be in order for us to measure the cause–effect relation efficiently. Without that careful specification, and with an arbitrary choice of time intervals, we do not know whether we are measuring the effect at its peak, its ebb, or somewhere in between. These and some related issues about temporal features of research methods are the focus of Chapter 6.

CHAPTER 7: TOWARD A SOCIAL PSYCHOLOGY OF TIME

The book ends with a chapter that summarizes key ideas, makes suggestions for a temporal language, and suggests ideas for potential future research that would build toward a full-fledged social psychology of time. Such a full-fledged "discipline" must take into account conceptual, substantive, and methodological material germane to its area of concern (i.e., to time) and we note how all three of these aspects are dealt with in the book. It must also share a common terminology for discussing time. We offer a set of definitions of temporal terms. Finally, we outline four areas of research that we feel would be especially fruitful in the development of a social psychology of time.

C H A P T E R   2

The Nature of Time

We began our study of time with the expectation that we would find very little prior work on it. That expectation proved to be both right and wrong. There indeed had been little work on temporal factors in what might be called "social psychology proper." But there had been a great deal of work on time in many surrounding fields. Work on time in philosophy stretched back more than 3 millennia. There was much on time in both classical and modern physics, a considerable amount in the biological sciences, and some in anthropology and sociology. There was also a substantial body of work in both experimental and clinical psychology, the former on the psychophysics of judgments of time and the latter on aberrations in those judgments. But there was really very little at a social-psychological level.

One early task of the program, therefore, was to try to get a working knowledge of how temporal concerns had been handled in some of those neighboring disciplines. Some of the results of that effort are noted here, far too briefly to reflect properly either their difficulty or their strategic place in our pursuit of a social psychology of time.

This chapter focuses on about a dozen major unresolved philosophical questions about time, issues such as whether time is to be considered continuous or divisible, objective or subjective, reversible or irreversible. These questions are not resolvable, in the sense of determining a correct answer. Rather, each culture adopts a set of value preferences for positions on these issues. The result, in any given time and place, is a culturally dominant conception of time and, perhaps, one or more variant conceptions. That dominant conception, and the variant conceptions as well, have a pervasive impact on the behavior of individuals within that culture.

The dominant conception of time in our culture, and several major potential variants, are examined in terms of those philosophical issues. To do so, we organize those issues into four clusters, having to do with the flow, the structure, the validity, and the reality of time. We represent each cluster of issues as a two-dimensional pattern, and regard each quadrant of that two-dimensional pattern as a potential "stance" that a conception of time could take on the issues underlying that cluster (i.e., flow, structure, validity, reality). The culturally dominant conception of time, and each of several major variant conceptions, is composed of one quadrant from each of the four clusters. The last two sections of this chapter present a discussion of the implications of several of these conceptions of time for human social behavior.

Some Unresolved Philosophical Issues

The work in the philosophy of time is both the most interesting and the most difficult to grasp. Much of the past work on the philosophy of time can be construed as a series of less than a dozen *unresolved philosophical questions about the nature of time* (as Heath, 1956, has done in her short but excellent book). For example: Is time divisible? Is it homogeneous or are some moments different from others? Is time objective or subjective? Is it singular or can there be more than one time?

From our perspective, these "unresolved philosophical questions" are unresolvable. They are issues for which there is not, and cannot be, a "right answer." Instead, they pose choices as to how humans can conceptualize time. Every culture (and subculture) develops preferred positions on each of these issues, and that set of value preferences determines how time will be construed within that culture. That construal, in turn, has broad and deep effects on the behavior of the individuals who are embedded within that culture.

We have organized a number of those unresolved philosophical questions about time into four major subsets or clusters. Each cluster addresses a different aspect of the matter. Those four clusters are: (1) the *validity* of definitions and measures of time; (2) the *structure* of time; (3) the *reality* of time; and (4) the *flow* of time.

THE VALIDITY OF TIME

One set of unresolved philosophical issues about time has to do with the validity of the construct of time and of its measures. These issues involve at least two sets of questions. One set has to do with what we might call the construct validity of time. These questions involve the relations among the concepts of time, space, motion, and change. At one extreme on this issue is the position that *space and motion are basic, and that time is derivative* (this is the position taken by Piaget). At the opposite end of this issue is the position that *the concept of time is fundamental* (along with space), *and necessary to the definition of motion and change.*

The other set of questions in the validity cluster deal with concepts familiar to social psychologists under the labels of convergent and discriminant validity of measures. Discriminant validity has to do with whether time, space, and motion are inherently confounded, or are conceptually independent even though they are often (but not necessarily always) confounded in operations used to measure them. Convergent validity has to do with whether time is to be considered a unitary or singular concept. If so, then we would expect, indeed demand, to find agreement or convergence among all measures that purport to be operational definitions of time, and we must devise some ways to adjudicate among those measures when they disagree. Instead, we could hold that there can be more than one valid time (e.g., as viewed from the perspective of different observers or instruments). If so, then while we would not demand convergence among measures of different times, we would have further questions about the scope and limits of each of these competing concepts of time, and about the validity of measures of each of them. Together, these sets of questions—about construct, convergent, and discriminant validity—constitute one major cluster of philosophical issues regarding time.

Time, Motion, and Change

Questions about the relations among time, motion, and change are both ancient and basic. Long ago, Heraclitus proferred the radical view that flux and motion and change are fundamental, whereas matter and structure and stability are illusion. That view was rejected by Democritus and other early Greeks in favor of a view in which matter and structure and stability were fundamental and fixed, whereas change was ephemeral and/or illusory. The latter view was favored by Aristotle, who was the channel for the major influence of Greek philosophy on the West. That Aristotle/Democritus view was also adopted by the major Western philosophers who were to dominate that culture and its developing science: Galileo, Descartes, Newton, Bacon, and the like. (Differences in the Democritus–Heraclitus views on these matters foreshadow differences between the views of classical physics and the "new physics" that will be discussed later in this chapter.)

To some extent, time has been defined in terms of movement, that is, change in location or position of objects in space. Conversely, motion has been defined in terms of change in location over time. Such definitions get one into lots of logical problems, including the implications of the well-known Heisenburg principle (which asserts the impossibility of measuring both the location and the momentum or velocity of a particle at the same time). (We should note, also, that the phrase, "at the same time," in the preceding sentence, is itself an interesting case in point about the complexity of temporal concepts.)

The matter is further complicated because there are some kinds of changes—changes in state, such as the change from water to ice—that do not involve any movement through space, or any change in location in space and that therefore may or may not involve time. For example, does ice form instantly, if temperature reaches 0° Celsius, or does it take time for ice to form? Even these changes, motionless at the relatively macro level of our direct observation, may involve changes in rates of molecular movement at micro levels of observation. And the very measurement of temperature itself may be done by measuring movement—of mercury, or of parts of a thermo-couple—over time.

One or Many Times?

Still another way to pose these questions about the relations among time, space, and motion is raised by the Heisenberg principle. The Heisenberg principle asserts that we cannot measure accurately both the position and the velocity of an object at the same time. To measure one requires that we disturb the other. Does that principle imply that time and motion and change are inherently confounded; or merely that, though conceptually distinct, measures of them are (often or always) operationally intertwined? Putting the matter in this form lets us translate some of the unresolved philosophical issues of this cluster into the kind of validity questions that are more familiar to us, such as: *Can time be measured validly* in the construct validity sense? If so, *can there be more than one valid time?*

The answers to these two questions indicate what our expectations ought to be about convergence among different measures of time. If there is but one true time, then when measures of time disagree, all measures of time that do not converge perfectly with that "true time" are "in error" and need to be corrected with reference to the true time. But Einsteinian ideas of relativity would seem to take sharp issue with that premise. In relativity theory, time as reckoned will differ as a function of the location and movement of both the observed and the observer. The idea of a singular "true time" against which all other measures are to be calibrated does not seem to square with this conception. This whole set of considerations, in turn, raises questions about the psychological experience of time. Some of those questions will be discussed later, in relation to another cluster of issues that involve objective versus subjective definitions of time.

THE STRUCTURE OF TIME

Another set of issues about the meaning of time has to do with *whether time is to be regarded as continuous or discontinuous*. One issue here is whether time is to be considered *holistically*, as one continuous "fabric," or, instead, is to be regarded atomistically, *as divisible*. Related to this issue is the question of whether time is to be considered *as pure duration* (as in the philosopher Bergson's concept of *durée real*), *or as succession* (i.e., as a series of successive instants). Still another related question is whether time is to be considered as "homogeneous" (i.e., each part identical to all other parts) or as "epochal" (i.e., certain "pieces" of time differing, qualitatively, from others). These three, together, make up a second cluster of questions, dealing with the structure of time.

If time is to be thought of as continuous and holistic, how then shall we measure it? But if time is to be thought of as atomistic and divisible, made up of tiny units strung together, then is there some "smallest possible particle" of time, some "temporal quark"? And *can there be temporal lacunae between those tiny temporal units*? On the face of it, this would seem an issue long settled in favor of the position that time is holistic, with divisions of it merely arbitrary and pragmatic. But some of the ideas of modern atomic physics, quantum theory, and relativity seem to pose the issues of units of time and their accurate measurement in new forms. These questions are also related to issues involving the psychological experience of time. For example, does the present overlap with the future and/or the past? Can there be "empty temporal spaces," experientially, between segments of time?

Another aspect of temporal structure is whether time is to be thought of as homogeneous, with each second like every other second, or as epochal, with some instants of time qualitatively different from other instants of time. This issue pits the universalistic and homogeneous aspect of time, viewed as an abstract reference dimension, against the particularistic and epochal aspect of time as we experience it in our daily lives. For many purposes it is convenient to act as if time is homogeneous, backward and forward. But it is also useful, sometimes, to regard certain "locations in time" as of special significance, either personally (e.g., my 21st birthday) or generically (e.g., the turn of the century). These issues obviously get entangled with the issues of the validity cluster, dealing with the measurement of time and its singularity. They also get involved with questions of the subjective experience of time that will be discussed as part of the next cluster.

THE REALITY OF TIME

Another set of temporal issues revolve around the question of time's realness or unrealness. One central question, here, is whether time is to be regarded as "absolute," existing independent of events, or as "relational," inhering in the relations among events and having no existence separate from them. One related question is whether time is to be viewed as "abstract," as "merely" a medium within which events occur, or as "concrete," in the sense of having real or tangible effects. Still another related question is whether time is to be regarded as "objective," "out there," or as "subjective," as existing "merely" (or essentially) in the psychological experience of the individual. These three questions are distinct, though related, and they all play into the central question of time's "realness," both within the universe and within human experience.

Time as Abstract or Concrete

Is time to be regarded as real, in the sense of being "concrete" and having direct effects, or is it to be regarded as not-real, in the sense of being only an "abstract" dimension? Mathematics and classical physical science seem to adopt the latter view, time as an abstract dimension with only a locational or reference function. The biological sciences (and, largely, the social sciences) seem to incorporate the former idea, that time is an essential ingredient in many life and behavioral processes (e.g., gestation, healing, metamorphosis).

This difference in conceptualization of time may also be related to another difference between the physical and biological sciences, that of how they treat the concept of "entropy." The physical sciences see entropy or randomness as always increasing over time. The biological sciences may see organization, structure and information, both within the organism and in the organism's relation to its environment, as increasing over time. Social psychology borrows perspectives from both physical and biological sciences, and is of two minds on the entropy concept as well.

Objective versus Subjective Time

Another way to consider this set of issues is to ask whether time is to be regarded as "relational," inhering in the relations between events, or as "absolute," independent of events and of the people involved in them. This is closely related, also, to the matter of time as objective or subjective. If there is an objective time, marked by rotations and orbits of the planets or oscillations of subatomic particles, then how does our human experience of time correspond with this? And, if the two are different, which one is to be regarded as correct?

The relation between objective and subjective time is one area in which psychologists—experimental and clinical—have made a major contribution to the study of time. There have been many studies done on "mapping" objective and subjective time (the psychophysics of time), and on finding conditions that distort such a "time sense" (e.g., fatigue, mental disorders, drugs, brain damage). But virtually all of that work, both clinical and experimental, is done on the premise that there is a singular, and known or knowable, objective time, and that the experience of time is to be examined in terms of accuracy and error in relation to that "true time." Virtually none of that work regards experienced time as the "true" time, to be taken as a criterion; nor does it regard the establishment of a "true" (objective) time as the least bit problematic, except in the trivial sense of keeping one's watch wound and set properly. But time in the "new physics" of Einsteinian relativity and quantum theory (and in some other conceptions as well) is far less clear-cut.

THE FLOW OF TIME

A final set of issues about time cluster around the central question of temporal flow. The key factor expressing this set of issues is often posed as the question of whether time is to be regarded as "linear" or as "cyclical." But that question confounds at least two others, closely related but not quite identical. One is the question of whether time is to be regarded as "uniform" or "phasic" in its passage. The other is the question of whether time is to be regarded as "unidirectional" or "bidirectional." A linear view of time implies both that time is directional and that it is uniform in its passage. A cyclical view of time implies that time is phasic in its passage, but does not require that it be either unidirectional or bidirectional. Together, these three questions, linearity versus cyclicality, uniformity of passage, and directionality, make up a cluster having to do with how time, in some general sense, flows.

Features of these conceptions are interdependent. If one treats time as an abstract dimension of human experience and of the universe, one is likely also to regard it as a continuous, homogeneous extension (or succession of instants), both forward and backward in time and without limit, from "the present." This view is, in general, the viewpoint of mathematics and classical physical science, though not of the "new physics" of Einsteinian relativity and quantum theory.

On the other hand, if one thinks of time in relation to life, one is apt to regard it as a "cycle"—a circle or a spiral—rather than as a line. A cyclic view seems appropriate at a "species level" (e.g., evolutionary change), at an "organism level" (e.g., the life cycle), and at a "daily-cycle level" (e.g., circadian rhythms). In those contexts, time seems to have a recurring, cyclical form. Winter comes, goes, and comes again. People live, die, and get born. There is a chicken-egg-chicken-egg progression. This view is, in general, the viewpoint of the biological sciences. Social psychology has borrowed conceptual paradigms extensively from both biological and classical physical sciences, and both linear and cyclical conceptions of time are embedded within it.

DOMINANT AND VARIANT CONCEPTIONS OF TIME

The issues just discussed are, on the one hand, unresolved questions in the philosophy of time; but they are also unresolvable metaphysical issues and epistemological dilemmas. Futhermore, each culture must have some view of time in terms of which its members carry on life and thought in that culture. For each culture, there is a set of preferred answers to those philosophical issues that constitutes the culturally dominant conception of time for that time and place. As cultures change, so do cultural conceptions of time—but usually quite slowly, as is the case for change in most value orientations. On the other hand, subcultures usually develop within each culture, and those subcultures hold variant cultural conceptions, including variants in the conception of time. We want to use the "unresolved philosophical issues" to help us examine the culturally dominant conception of time in our culture, and some important subcultural variants.

The culturally dominant view of time in the lay culture of the United States and most of the Western world is the one derived from classical mathematics and physics (with one modification, to be discussed later). This view, which we will call "Newtonian" time, has dominated both Western lay culture and the classical sciences that have grown up within it. There are several sets of ideas that constitute major potential alternatives to our "classical" ideas about time. These may eventually emerge as clear-cut subcultural variants, but really have not yet crystallized into a coherent view. One is the set of ideas about time that derives from what has been called the "new physics." We put that term in quotation marks because the physics in question is nearly a century old now—thermodynamics and entropy, relativity, quantum theory, the Heisenberg principle, and so forth. What is "new"—and indeed still incipient—is the impact of the underlying premises of that new physics on either the social sciences or the lay culture, in regard to conceptions of time as well as other matters. So that subculture provides some features, but not yet a complete and coherent conception, of time. If the dominant conception is Newtonian, this variant conception is Einsteinian.

Another major set of variations in views of time arise in part from some issues within the biological sciences. But here, too, we are talking about a "new biology" rather than the classical ideas in that field (which are very Newtonian). Here, also, the emerging view of time has neither yet had much impact on the lay culture nor yet been clearly crystallized into a coherent view of time. In psychology and other social sciences, this view has to some degree been associated with organismic or Transactional perspectives.

There are still other variant conceptions of time, some reflecting lay cultures other than our own. One especially prominent one is the conception of time that arises from cultures of the Far East and reflects a combination of the philosophy, religion, and science of those cultures. Capra (1975) refers to this conception as Eastern mysticism. He regards that view of time as really quite close to the one that is emerging from the new physics; we do not agree. In terms of our framework, the Eastern philosophies provide still a fourth more or less coherent conception of time that stands as a potential major variant to the classical conception of our culture.

We want to use the four clusters of unresolved philosophical issues, discussed in the preceding section, as a basis for systematically examining those four conceptions of time: the dominant cultural conception that arises from classical Newtonian physical science, and that (with one modification) permeates the lay culture still; and the three major variants reflecting time as conceived in the "new physics," in the biological sciences, and in the philosophies of the cultures of the Far East. We will label those conceptions of time, in the diagrams and discussion to follow, as: (1) the classical or scientific or Newtonian paradigm, (2) the new physics or Einsteinian paradigm, (3) the Transactional or biological paradigm, and (4) the Eastern mysticism paradigm.

We will view each cluster of issues as a two-dimensional region whose main axes are defined by two of the basic philosophical issues previously discussed, with other issues embedded within that region. The names we have given the issues reflected by each cluster, and the questions defining their main axes, are listed here:

I. The Structure of Time
   a. Is time to be regarded: (1) as holistic, indivisible; or (2) as atomistic, divisible?
   b. Is time to be regarded: (1) as homogeneous, each instant the same as any other; or (2) as containing qualitative differentiations?
II. The Flow of Time
   a. Is time to be regarded: (1) as bidirectional or reversible; or (2) as unidirectional or irreversible in its flow?
   b. Is time to be regarded: (1) as flowing uniformly; or (2) as phasic in its passage?
III. The Reality of Time
   a. Is time to be regarded: (1) as absolute, existing independent of objects and events; or (2) as relational, inhering in the relations among objects and events?
   b. Is time to be regarded: (1) as abstract, as "merely" a dimension along which events can be represented; or (2) as concrete, having existentially real effects?
IV. The Validity of Time
   a. Is time to be regarded: (1) as singular, with one and only one "correct" time; or (2) as multiple, with potentially more than one "correct" time?
   b. Is time to be regarded: (1) as independent of space and motion (though sometimes confounded with them in the measurement process); or (2) as inherently con-

founded with space and motion and/or derived from them (as is implied in the logic of the Heisenberg principle)?

The four clusters are shown in Figures 2-1 through 2-4. Note that in each of the four quadrants near the crossing point of the main axes, there is a designation of one (or more) of the time conceptions of which that quadrant is a part. All four of the plots are oriented so that the classical Newtonian conception of time appears as the northwest quadrant, but the other three conceptions do not occur in a fixed position.

THE CLASSICAL NEWTONIAN TEMPORAL PARADIGM

The dominant way in which people living in our culture conceptualize time is, with one modification, the conception of time that was developed as the backbone of the classical physical sciences. It seems appropriate to call it the Newtonian paradigm. While this is no longer the conception of time that drives the advanced physical sciences (e.g., particle physics), it is still nevertheless largely the conception that dominates the lay cultures of the industrialized nations of Western civilization. In this Newtonian conception, classical physical science viewed time as: atomistic (divisible) but homogeneous (not differentiated), and therefore as succession; abstract and absolute (independent of objects) and therefore as mathematical time, so to speak; linear (uniform in flow) and reversible, therefore as bidirectional; and as a singular independent dimension, hence high in both convergent and discriminant validity (i.e., time can be measured as a valid independent construct, and all good measures of it will converge except for errors of measurement).

The dominant view of time in our lay culture departs from the Newtonian conception only in regard to time's irreversibility. The irreversibility of transformations in thermodynamics (and the consequent inevitable increase in entropy) was one of the first outcroppings of the "new physics" (Prigogine & Stengers, 1984), and the only one as yet incorporated into the

HOMOGENEOUS
(Undifferentiated)
Time as
SUCCESSION
Time as
DURATION
ATOMISTIC
(Divisible)
Classical
Transactional
Eastern
Einsteinian
HOLISTIC
(Indivisible)
Time as
EPOCHAL
Time as
TRANSPOSABLE
DIFFERENTIATED

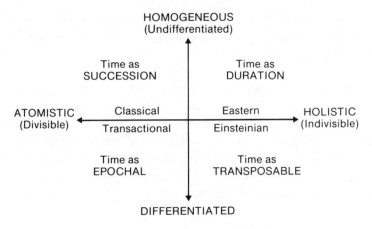

Figure 2-1. The structure of time.

lay culture's dominant temporal paradigm. The enormous impact of this conception of time on our culture will be examined in the next section of this chapter, on clocks and calendars.

THE TIME CONCEPTION OF THE NEW PHYSICS

One major potential variant to this culturally dominant conception is the one that seems to be emerging from what Capra

Figure 2-2. The flow of time.

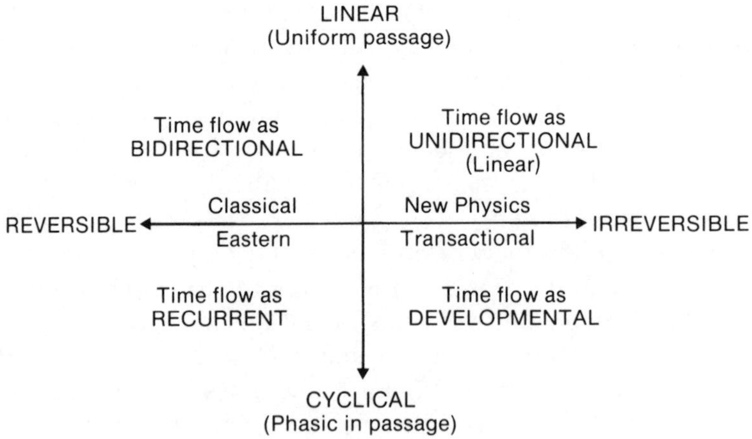

LINEAR
(Uniform passage)
Time flow as
BIDIRECTIONAL
Time flow as
UNIDIRECTIONAL
(Linear)
REVERSIBLE
Classical
Eastern
New Physics
Transactional
IRREVERSIBLE
Time flow as
RECURRENT
Time flow as
DEVELOPMENTAL
CYCLICAL
(Phasic in passage)

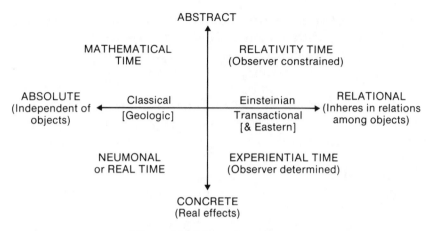

Figure 2-3. The reality of time.

(1975) has called the "new physics," and what Prigogine and Stengers (1984) call the "science of complexity": thermodynamics, relativity theory, atomic theory, quantum mechanics, and other advanced work in modern physics. That time conception is not yet altogether clear, since it has not yet emerged as a coherent cultural or subcultural interpretation of time (even for the daily, nonprofessional lives of the community of physicists on the "leading edge" of that field). Generally, though, it builds on the following conception: In terms of structure,

Figure 2-4. The validity of time.

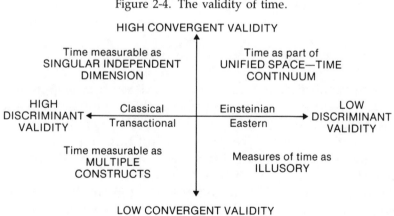

thanks to quantum theory, time is regarded as in some sense indivisible but differentiated. This idea is similar to the transformations between wave and pulse representations that seem to characterize quantum physics. To this feature, we have linked the term "transposability." Physicists sometimes use the term "complementarity" to refer to this same transformability. In regard to reality, time is regarded as abstract but relational (à la Einstein's relativity), with the viewpoint of the observer constituting an integral feature of the measurement of time. With respect to flow, time is regarded as uniform in its passage, but irreversible or unidirectional in its flow (as in thermodynamic's "arrow of time" that yields ever-increasing entropy). As to its validity, in Einsteinian physics, time is regarded as inherently a part of a unified, four-dimensional space–time continuum. Hence, measures of time would be expected to have low discriminant but high convergent validity (i.e., measures of time are convergent, but are not sharply differentiated from measures of space and motion, as in the Heisenberg Principle). If the dominant conception of time, discussed above, is to be called Newtonian, then this one rightly ought to be called Einsteinian. (It is an irony that the irreversibility of time is the only feature of the "new physics" that has become an important part of the time conception of the lay culture; and it is the only part of that "Einsteinian time" that was not acceptable to Einstein. According to Prigogine & Stengers, 1984, Einstein regarded time as irreversible only in a phenomenological sense.)

THE BIOLOGICAL OR TRANSACTIONAL TIME PARADIGM

Another conception of time that could serve as a potential major variant of the time conception that dominates our lay culture reflects the thinking that derives from certain issues in the biological sciences. These issues and this time conception arise in what one might call the "new biology" (parallel to the idea of the "new physics"), rather than in classical biology, which, by and large, followed the Newtonian classical conception in regard to time as well as in regard to other features of the scientific paradigm. This "new biology" view pays special attention to periodic or cyclical phenomena in living systems at various levels (cells, organisms, species, etc.), and to the mutual entrainment of these oscillatory processes. It is a view of time that could also be regarded as the temporal paradigm for a Transactional conception of behavior.

The biological or Transactional view has the following conception of time: In regard to structure, time is divisible but differentiated, with certain points in time serving as "critical values" (e.g., birth, metamorphosis, cell division, etc.). Therefore, time is experienced as epochal. With respect to reality, time is regarded as concrete, in that it is a necessary ingredient of many biological processes. It is also regarded as relational. Therefore, it is an experiential time that is in part observer determined. In regard to flow, time is considered as phasic in passage, and irreversible. Therefore it is developmental in its flow, spiral in form rather than strictly recurrent. In regard to validity, if time is to be viewed as experiential, partly observer determined, then there must potentially be multiple valid time constructs. Therefore, measures of time will not necessarily be marked by high convergence with all other measures of time. But measures of each of those separate "times" nevertheless *can* have high discriminant validity. That is, the separate times can each be validly measured, independently of other constructs such as space and motion, although measures of those separate time constructs will not necessarily converge with one another. The biological or Transactional conception will be discussed further in a later section of this chapter, on cycles, rhythms, and entrainment.

THE TEMPORAL PARADIGM OF EASTERN MYSTICISM

It is even more difficult to talk about the fourth time conception, reflected in some of the remaining quadrants. This conception of time is embedded within a number of Eastern philosophies. Capra (1975) considers the paradigm of Eastern mysticism, in general, to be convergent with the one he sees as emerging from the "new physics." We are not in agreement with that interpretation, at least in regard to those aspects of the respective paradigms that are related to time.

In any case, our interpretation of the conception of time in Eastern philosophies is as follows: In regard to structure, time is viewed as indivisible and homogeneous, hence is represented as duration or extension. In regard to flow, time is viewed as phasic but reversible. Hence, time is cyclical in the sense of strict recurrence rather than in the sense of developmental spirals (there is some aspects of the developmental spiral in Eastern mysticism, however, in that there is movement toward an ideal state of being). In regard to validity, all measures of time are considered as inherently illusory. This reflects low convergent validity and also low discriminant validity. In this view, there are no good measures of time; measures of time do not converge with one another, and they are at the same time inherently confounded with measures of other constructs. In regard to reality, time is viewed as concrete and relational, hence experiential—a conception shared by the Eastern philosophies and the Transactional view. (The remaining fourth quadrant of this cluster, representing a time that is absolute and concrete, is a part of still another paradigm that we call "geological time." That view reflects a conception of time as independent of relations among objects and events, but as "marking" such objects and events in a variety of ways.)

SUMMARY

The "location" of each of these four conceptions of time, or temporal paradigms, within the four clusters of epistemological issues, are summarized in Table 2-1. There are potentially many other variant conceptions of time. In fact, this framework offers the possibility of 256 combinations consisting of one quadrant from each of the four clusters. We noted above a fifth one, that we called "geologic time." It fits into the otherwise unused ("real" time) quadrant of the reality cluster; it shares the Newtonian conception regarding validity and structure; and it shares the Einsteinian conception regarding flow. We have also mentioned the culturally dominant view, as a variant of the New-

Table 2-1. Major Conceptions of Time

	Clusters of temporal issues			
	Structure	Flow	Reality	Validity
Major temporal paradigms				
Newtonian	Succession	Bidirectional	Mathematical	Singular independent dimension
Einsteinian	Transposable	Unidirectional	Relativity	Unified space–time continuum
Transac-tional	Epochal	Developmental	Experiential	Multiple constructs
Eastern	Duration	Recurrent	Experiential	Illusory
Mixed paradigms				
Dominant cultural	Succession	Unidirectional	Mathematical	Singular independent dimension
Geologic	Succession	Unidirectional	Real Time	Singular independent dimension
Organiza-tional	Succession and epochal	Developmental and unidirectional	Mathematical	Singular independent dimension

tonian paradigm in regard to irreversibility. In the next chapter, we will also discuss another mixed variant, related to the technological tasks of many work settings, that we will call "organizational time." Those three are also included in Table 2-1. However, the four conceptions that we have outlined here—Newtonian, Einsteinian, Transactional, and Eastern— constitute the major contrasting temporal paradigms currently prominent in Western thought. The four clusters of epistemological issues regarding time, and the four main temporal paradigms, will provide a conceptual underpinning for the remainder of the book. Sometimes we will make use of these four conceptions to clarify a particular issue; sometimes we will use them to pose new questions in regard to a seemingly well-understood issue.

The next two sections of this chapter will elaborate on three of these four temporal paradigms. The "clocks and calendars" section deals with the dominance of Newtonian thought in our measures of the passage of time. It also deals with some of the challenges to this position that have grown out of modern physics—that is, the Einsteinian conception of time. The final section of this chapter, on "cycles, rhythms, and entrainment," deals with the treatment of time in the life sciences. That section deals, in particular, with the cyclical nature of many biological processes, and suggests the possibility of phasic, rather than uniform, processes in many social behaviors. Those latter ideas, regarding rhythms of social behavior and the social entrainment of such rhythms, are key concepts in later chapters of the book.

Clocks and Calendars:
The Culture's Dominant Conception of Time

By and large, when people think of time they think of *clocks and calendars*. And clocks and calendars embody premises about almost all of the temporal issues discussed in the preceding sections. In the lay culture, time is thought of as both linear and cyclical; clocks and calendars imply both. We tend to *think about time* as of it were abstract, unidirectional, uniform in passage, divisible, and homogeneous; but we tend to *use time* as if it were concrete, phasic, and epochal. In our major symbolic systems, time is usually represented as continuous but with infinitely divisible units, hence as a succession of instants rather than as duration or extension. Generally, in the lay culture, time is considered inherently measurable—literally, *time inheres in its measure*—and as objective, singular, and accurately knowable. The clock (or sundial) ties the measurement of time to motion, although the calendar does not.

The salience of clocks and calendars in our images of time makes it clear that our culture's dominant conception of time is heavily influenced by classical (essentially Newtonian) physical science and mathematics. Calendars rely largely on properties of the astronomical world: years, months, and days are *loosely* coupled to major planetary events. Clocks rely largely on a mathematical view of time, with abstract, uniform, arbitrary divisions of the basic calendar unit, the day. We tend to use abstract, homogeneous, substantively "empty," arbitrary time units at a micro level (hours, minutes, seconds, microseconds, etc.) and at the very macro level (decades, centuries, and beyond). In contrast, we tend to use planetary movements, with a cyclical and epochal character, for time units in the middle range of months, seasons, and years.

The day and the week are mixed cases. The day is both our astronomical and our bio-behavioral unit. Not only does it mark one turn of the earth about its axis (or, as held in earlier times, one turn of the sun about the earth); it also marks one day–night, dark–light, sleep–wake cycle for the human, animal, and vegetable inhabitants of that planet.

A week is a very special case. It is currently a 7-day cycle, but at other times and places it has ranged from 3 to 10 days. A week has neither uniform mathematical properties, nor clear astronomical connections. Nor does it have direct biological connections. Rather, it has *social and economic* import. The concept is derived from a term originally related to the periodicity of "markets"—opportunities to trade for food and other goods. Therefore, its duration was related to both food preservation and transportation technologies. In Judeo-Christian cultures, the week acquired religious significance as well (i.e., the biblical 7-day creation cycle). In recent times, it has acquired a new form of economic significance, as the vehicle for pacing work and nonwork periods (i.e., definitions of a week of workdays and a weekend of nonwork days).

THE MEASUREMENT OF TIME

The history of the technology for measurement of time is instructive. It points out how intimately our concepts and our measures are intertwined. The measurement of time involves inventing devices that will automatically track some continuous—or uniformly paced—process, and that will automatically display the status of that tracking (either continuously or intermittently). The crux of the matter is to carry out that tracking and displaying with sufficient accuracy for the intended purposes, and to do so in a way that retains accuracy over time with a minimum of maintenance (e.g., winding of a clock or inverting of an hourglass).

One early form of such tracking–displaying was a sundial. Here, what is "tracked" is the (continuous) movement of the earth in relation to the sun; and the display is in the form of a projection of shadow on a circular plane. The mapping of movement to position of the shadow varies as a function of location on the earth's surface and the seasons of the year, but both of these functions are systematic and knowable, and thus can be taken into account with great precision. Otherwise, the sundial needs little maintenance to retain its accuracy forever. The sundial is an ideal timekeeper, except for four limitations: It is not precise enough for some purposes (for example, to time a footrace); it does not work at night; it is not portable; and its display cannot be read from a distance.

Other early forms of time keeping were based on continuous processes that relied on the force of gravity operating on a "pile" of homogeneous material. Water clocks, for example, rely on the uniformity of flow of water, either into or out of a vessel, through an opening of known size. Hourglasses rely, in the same way, on the flow of uniform particles of sand through a fixed opening from one chamber to another. Both water clocks and hourglasses are far more portable than sundials, can be made to be more precise, and do work at night. But they require continuous resetting; hence they lose their accuracy over extended periods of time. And they, too, cannot be read at a distance.

The time-keeping systems we know as clocks make use of any of a number of physical processes: the gravitational pull on known weights; the unwinding of springs (which is nonuniform over time and thus needs both winding and correcting); and the oscillation of pendula. In all of these, what is "tracked" is some form of movement, automatic once set in motion but requiring some degree of maintenance for continuing accuracy. Time keeping by clocks improved as devices were developed to control that movement (and/or correct it) with greater and greater precision. One key device for such control was the "escapement," an ingenious principle for translating such automatic mechanical force into regulated oscillations of a balance wheel. The escapement, in its various forms, was the basis for order-of-magnitude advances in continuing accuracy, precision, and portability of clocks.

Some early clocks, used in monastic life, "displayed" time only in auditory form, by means of bells signaling a particular time of day. While sounds signaling the hours and their parts continued to be a part of large clocks (thus making the clock's display "readable" over rather long distances), all later clocks have relied mainly on a visual display. Until quite recently, these have almost all been in the form of center-anchored, rotating marker(s) (i.e., hands) on a circular dial.

In modern times, time-keeping technology has shifted from devices that track mechanical movement and display it as angular rotation on a circular surface (i.e., a "clock") to devices that abstract the oscillations of certain atomic or subatomic particles of known frequency. The display of such oscillations could be done in any of a variety of forms; but currently it is almost always done as a *digital* display of a number that represents a *succession* of some temporal unit that is a submultiple of a "day." For example, the display might represent a millisecond, which is the $1000 \times 60 \times 60 \times 24$th part of an "accurately measured day."

We have come a long way indeed in our operational definitions of time. With the atomic clock, we no longer define a given temporal unit, such as a millisecond, by slicing up a solar day. Instead, we establish that temporal unit in terms of the oscillation frequency of the chosen element (e.g., cesium), and then define an "exact day" by adding up those micro units (e.g., $1000 \times 60 \times 60 \times 24$ milliseconds). We are thereby regarding the arbitrary and abstract unit for measuring micro time as the *accurate standard* against which to correct or calibrate the relatively inaccurate, though "natural," unit that we call a day. By so doing, we have redefined time as *atomistic succession*, rather than as *holistic duration*. Moreover, the powerfully accurate atomic clock now is used to correct for changes in the time contained within the "natural" unit of a year that come about because of a *slowing of the motion of the planet*. So what was initially an arbitrary submultiple of time measures, referring to essentially "natural" units (a day, a year), now serves as *the criterion—and master—of time*, and of motion and change in the universe.

Thus, far from being merely the instrumental means for measuring time—regarded either in the abstract or as a property of astronomical events in the universe—mathematics and the physical sciences have become the basis for establishing, or at least altering, our conceptual as well as our operational definitions for time.

TIME AND THE "NEW PHYSICS"

There have been profound changes in the conceptions underlying the physical sciences, beginning toward the end of the 19th century. At present, those fields are on the verge of what seems to some to be a wholly new metaphysics (cf. Capra, 1975; Prigogine & Stengers, 1984). That new world view has been considered to be, in some respects, akin to the view of Eastern philosophies (Capra, 1975). In any case, it is quite alien to the previously dominant world view of classical physics, to most current Western philosophies, and to Western lay cultures.

In principle, these new ideas imply radical changes for the classical conception of time that has dominated both classical physical sciences and the lay culture of the Western world. But they have gained sway in only the most advanced parts even of theoretical physics. They have not yet begun to dominate the way most scientists think about time. And, except for the one issue of time's irreversibility, they have as yet had little impact on the conception of time that dominates the lay culture.

At the same time, this ferment and these avant garde changes let us raise issues about our conceptions of time that have been unthinkable for many years because of the procrustean power of the dominant Newtonian cultural view of time throughout that period. In particular, several major advances in modern physics have raised anew many of the seemingly resolved issues in the philosophy of time.

First, thermodynamics called into question the *reversibility* of Newtonian time, and replaced it—*even in the lay culture*—with an *irreversible, directional* time, leading to increased entropy. Second, Einstein's relativity, and related issues such as the Heisenberg principle, raise anew the long-resolved question of whether there can be more than one time, and if so how do we adjudicate among measures of them. Those ideas also resurrect ancient concerns about the relations of time, motion, and change. For example, if we are to regard time–space as a unitary, four-dimensional continuum, what then is motion? And what is aging?

Modern quantum physics raises still more disturbing questions, about the stability and even the existence of material objects within that time–space continuum. Heraclitus would not be a radical among today's advanced theoretical physicists. Both relativity theory and quantum physics would also seem to question the degree to which we can regard time differentials as marking smooth, uniform changes (as contrasted with phasic or oscillatory ones).

At the same time, some of those involved in the new physics (e.g., those searching for the elusive quarks) still seem to be searching for some smallest particles, some basic building blocks within which we can find neither differentiated structure nor divisibility. What of the divisibility of time? Perhaps time is not *infinitely* divisible. Perhaps there is a lower bound for time units, a smallest temporal particle, a temporal quark. If so, then perhaps time may be less homogeneous, more epochal, than we have generally regarded it. This would leave open the possibility of temporal gaps, lacunae, however tiny, between those tiny but finite particles of time.

These are fascinating problems, though still far removed from the social-psychological level at which we set out to work. But this discussion suggests some of the unfinished complexity of the temporal topic, even those parts of it we thought long settled. Some additional disturbing questions arise when we look at time from the perspective of the biological sciences, our next task.

Cycles, Rhythms, and Entrainment: Views of Time in the Life Sciences

The view of time taken by classical physical sciences, modified with regard to its irreversibility, is also the culturally dominant view permeating virtually all aspects of Western culture and its institutions (e.g., its organizations, governments, humanities, socioeconomic structures, and so forth). Even though there are some new ideas now in fashion in modern physics that seem to challenge the classical view of time, this new world view has not yet reached, let alone come to dominate, the general culture (or even the physical sciences themselves).

But during much of the time that the Newtonian view of time has been the dominant cultural view, there has been one major counterpointal view of time. That counterview arises from some special features of the biological organisms that populate the planet. (The biological sciences themselves grew up "in the shadow of" the immensely successful and powerful classical physical sciences, and have been duly embedded within the culture dominated by that classical view. Hence, this counterpointal conception of time represents what Kluckhohn & Strodtbeck, 1961, called a subcultural "variant" of the dominant culture.)

Some of those special features of biological organisms have already been alluded to in the discussion of the major philosophical issues regarding time. One striking feature is the importance of endogenous cycles, oscillations or rhythms within biological processes. A second striking feature is the operation of "entrainment processes," by which one cyclic process becomes "captured" by, and set to oscillate in rhythm with, another. The importance of such cycles and rhythms within living organisms, and of their entrainment to other internal cycles and external pacers, makes a phasic view of time much more attractive in biological fields than in mathematics.

A biological view of time differs from a mathematical view in some other ways as well. For example, many biological processes seem to involve temporal features that are epochal, and certainly nonhomogeneous, in form: birth, death, metamorphosis. Furthermore, a biological view is much more likely than a mathematical view to tolerate the idea that time is relational, and has real (i.e., concrete) effects. (Time, after all, does heal all wounds.) And at least some biological perspectives might honor the idea of multiple and subjective times. But, above all, it is the cycles and their entrainment that give the biological sciences a special temporal character.

Recurrent cycles are indeed highly salient features of human behavior. Many aspects of our lives are influenced by cycles tied to the planet's activity within the solar system (e.g., the day–night cycle, seasons of the year). Many others are influenced by biological rhythms from within ourselves (e.g., temperature cycles; activity–rest cycles; and other circadian, infradian, and ultradian rhythms of many sorts). The latter cycles tend to be in mutual synchrony, or mutual entrainment, with one another. They also can become entrained to outside "pacers" or *zeitgebers* (time givers) as well.

ENTRAINMENT

In biological study, the term "entrainment" means, roughly, that an endogenous body rhythm has been "captured," and modified in its periodicity and its phase, by an external cycle with a rhythm near to the one the body rhythm would have had (in its "natural" endogenous form) had it not been thus captured and modified.

This idea is often illustrated by analogy to the action of one tuning fork on another. If a tuning fork is set in motion by an outside force and then held near another tuning fork of approximately the same frequency (or a multiple or submultiple of that frequency), it will set that second tuning fork into motion as well. We can say that the latter fork is entrained by (set in motion by) that first tuning fork.

The analogy has its limits, as is the case with most analogies. For one thing, the rhythms of the body are "endogenous"; they occur whether or not there is an "outside tuning fork," so to speak. In the case of the tuning fork, its "rhythm" lies dormant until an outside force occurs. The analogy is limited further because, in the case of the biological process, its endogenous rhythm is modified to the periodicity of the "outside tuning fork"; whereas that is not the case for the tuning fork. Furthermore, we know little about whether the newly adopted rhythm (entrained by the outside force) places a stress on the biological system supporting that process, or whether the ill effects of that stress are terminated when the outside entraining force is removed. In the case of the tuning fork, we assume no ill effects of its having been entrained "out of rhythm" for a time, and certainly no continuing ill effects. Such a presumption, of no effects or aftereffects, is surely unwarranted for the human biological system.

Pittendrigh argues that the problem of understanding the "mutual entrainment" of biological rhythms is the central problem for understanding organization in biological systems (Pittendrigh, 1972). He argues further that the body contains many rhythmic processes, at various temporal orders (microseconds, minutes, hours, months, years), and *that biological organization is the synchronization of all of those processes via mutual entrainment* (and, presumably, via some external entrainment as well). To be redundant, the cycles or rhythms themselves are "endogenous"—they go on whether or not they are in synchrony with any other cycles and whether or not they are in the presence of any outside cyclic forces. What is modified, by proximity to other internal or external rhythms, is not their occurrence but their *periodicity* and their *phase* (that is, what they are in synchronization with).

CIRCADIAN RHYTHMS

The particular biological cycles most often used to exemplify entrainment are the circadian rhythms that become entrained to the day–night cycle of life on planet Earth. There are a number of bodily cycles that exhibit a "natural" periodicity of approximately, but not exactly, 24 hours under so-called free-running conditions (when the effects of the "outside rhythm," the day–night cycle, have been removed—hence the name *circadian*, which is from two Latin words meaning "about" and "a day"). Those free-running cycles vary in periodicity from one individual to another, but are extremely regular for any one individual under free-running conditions. Under normal conditions of life on Earth, when the outside forces of the day–night cycle have not been removed, those circadian rhythms become "entrained" to, and operate in synchronization with, that day–night cycle.

For lower order biological species, the entraining power of the day–night rotation lies in two main parameters of that cycle: the *light–dark pattern* and the *temperature pattern*. Humans, on the other hand, are not so much affected by the natural changes in darkness and in temperature that accompany the Earth's daily rotation. After all, the maximum temperature range from noon to midnight on a summer day is far less than the variation in temperatures involved in going from outdoors to indoors on a winter's day. In any case, humans have elaborate temperature regulatory systems that function to maintain a relatively constant internal temperature quite distinct from the ambient temperature. *But body temperature itself fluctuates cyclically*, and is one of the circadian rhythms. Human body temperature normally is lowest during the night (3 to 5 A.M.), rises rapidly for the next 6 or 7 hours, rises more slowly until its peak around 8 or 9 P.M., then drops off linearly to its nighttime low. This temperature cycle, under normal conditions, is in synchronization with overall activity levels (which are also generally circadian in form), and with many circadian and ultradian (i.e., subcircadian) physiological cycles as well.

At the physiological level, sleep, activity, and many other physiological processes (e.g., some features of the cardiovascular, endocrine, and respiratory systems, and of urinary flow), each with its own endogenous rhythms, become synchronized with or *mutually entrained* to one another, rather than one or more of them being entrained to outside cycles such as the Earth's day–night rotation. But it is clear that such synchronization, or lack of it, among these temperature, activity, and other physiological cycles, has dramatic implications for much of human health and well-being, as well as for effectiveness of task and role performance.

What happens to those temperature and other cycles when the day–night pattern is modified for the individual? Such modification happens, for example, whenever people travel east–west through time zones, especially when the traveling is done at a rate much faster than the rotation takes place (as in jet travel). It also happens when people work night, evening, or rotating shifts.

There are apparently several effects. One is a decoupling of the temperature, activity, and other cycles, from "clock time on the ground," so to speak. This gradually gets restored, though not completely, within the first few days. A second effect is a desynchronization among the various body rhythms, including the temperature cycle. Another way to look at this effect is to consider it the consequence of *differential rates of adaptation to the time changes (re-entrainment) by different body rhythms*. During this desynchronization period, various body rhythms that are normally in synchrony are *out of phase with one another*. There is such a de-synchrony, for example, between body temperature and activity cycles (and indeed, among different aspects of those activity cycles). Third, there is also a modification not only of the phase and periodicity of the temperature (and other) cycles, but of their *amplitude* as well. In general, the amplitudes of both the temperature and activity cycles flatten during the adaptation period.

Sleep–wake cycles are also a part of this de-synchronization and adaptation picture. Sleep disturbances seem to operate, at one and the same time, as a forcing function for, as markers of, and as consequences of, these de-synchronization and adaptation phenomena. Sleep patterns, and disturbances in them, have been the subject of much study by both physiologists and psychologists.

One points needs to be emphasized here: Whereas the endogenous biological rhythms of plants and many lower order animals are strongly entrained to the dark–light and warm–cold cycles per se, humans are not. Rather, humans show quite strong patterns of mutual entrainment among their many endogenous rhythms—temperature, cardiovascular, excretory, activational—and all of these are also often entrained to exogenous cycles in the human's environment. (The mutual entrainment of human circadian rhythms is discussed in more detail later in the book).

The apparent entrainment of human endogenous rhythms to day–night cycles is largely a social-psychological rather than a biological matter. Whether either dark–light or warm–cold variations per se have any effects as entrainment agents for humans is still a matter requiring further research (cf. Moore-Ede, Sulzman, & Fuller, 1982). What is clear is that we certainly are strongly entrained to a culturally defined cycle of day and night (and to other culturally defined cycles as well), rather than to an astronomically defined cycle whose crucial features are light and temperature per se. Even in regard to physiological levels, *what is crucial is the mutual entrainment of endogenous cycles,* with their external entrainment to a day–night rotation quite arbitrary, though powerful once attained.

ENTRAINMENT OF PSYCHOLOGICAL PROCESSES

Entrainment applies to psychological as well as physiological processes. One important case in point pertains to judgments of the duration of current and past time intervals. Estimates of time become entrained to both internal and external periodicities, and these entrainments can be coupled, uncoupled, and altered in a number of ways. (For reviews, see Doob, 1971; McGrath & Rotchford, 1983; Ornstein, 1969; see also, Chapter 3). Subjective estimates of the passage of time are underestimated as temperature decreases (Bell, 1965; Hoagland, 1935). They are overestimated when stimulant drugs are administered (Fischer, 1966); and vary as a function of a number of other conditions. Subjective time lengthens with increases in the amount of information "stored" in long-term memory (Ornstein, 1969). Amount stored, in turn, varies with both external factors (e.g., amount and rate of external stimulation presented) and internal ones (e.g., efficiency of encoding and depth of cognitive processing). The perception of the passage of time, therefore, like many other individual processes and behaviors, is a function of endogenous rhythms that become mutually entrained with other physiological and psychological rhythms, and that also become entrained to exogenous signals or cycles in the individual's external environment. Such internal and external entrainment of time judgments may play a crucial role in the rather dramatic impact that temporal scarcity and abundance seem to have on social interaction and task performance. These matters are the topic of later chapters of this book.

ENTRAINMENT AND SOCIAL BEHAVIOR

Much of human behavior at the social-psychological level, and much behavior in group and organizational settings, also involves such mutual entrainment of endogenous rhythms, and these, too, become heavily entrained to quite arbitrary, but quite powerful, external cycles (i.e., work schedules, assigned task time limits, the standard cultural definitions of the seasons, social definitions of day and night times, workdays and weekends, and the like). The concept of (mutual and external) entrainment of multiple endogenous rhythms will be central to our discussion of research on time in several later chapters of this book. It is such *temporal entrainment of social and organizational behavior*—as distinct from the entrainment of physiological and psychological processes—that is of central concern within a social psychology of time.

C H A P T E R 3

Time and Human Experience

However the philosophers may argue about time, and however the scientists may conceptualize it in their theories, time is very prominent in the lives of human beings. Furthermore, time *as experienced* has many facets, many nuances, many ramifications. This chapter is about how time is experienced in human life.

The preceding chapter can be regarded as an "outside in" view of time. It considered time from a stance that is essentially at a universal level and laid out some temporal paradigms from that perspective. Here, we are going to try to bring that abstract view of time down to a more concrete level of human experience. This chapter will present an "inside out" view of time, from a stance that takes the perspective of an individual.

The chapter has two themes. First we explore the concept of "multiple times"—the myriad time frames within which individuals can "locate" themselves at any given instant. Then we turn to an examination of what is undoubtedly the temporal topic most studied by psychologists: namely studies of judgments of the passage of time (the so-called psychophysics of time). From our perspective this material is of special interest because the very question that it explores—how does the passing of "objective" time get translated into the experience of "subjective" time—is based on a comparison involving two different conceptions of time (the Newtonian and the Transactional).

A NETWORK OF TIME FRAMES

What time is it? That is a complex question. Today is Saturday, 29 June 1985 (A.D.) by the currently fashionable Gregorian calendar, but it is a different day in a different year by a number of other possible calendars: Hebrew, Julian, ancient Egyptian, Eastern Orthodox, Druid. It is also a certain day in the life of the planet Earth, in the life of the solar system and galaxy of which that planet is a part, and in the life of the human species. And here, again, we have a number of alternative "calendars" from which to choose, some religious and some scientific. It is also a certain day (the dth day) in a certain year (the nth year) of our lives—a different one for each of us, of course.

Regarding time of day, it is approximately 3:45 P.M. (or 15:45), U.S. Eastern Daylight Savings Time, to follow the currently fashionable way in which time is tracked in *this* time and place, in western Michigan (where this is first being set into words), although it is (was) only 2:45 P.M. in central Illinois or 12:45 P.M. in Seattle, Washington (at which locations other parts of this book were drafted). It is a still different time of day for people located in other places. And time of day is equivocal for someone who is aloft in an airplane that took off in one time zone and will land in another.

We could, of course, map all of these differences onto a common time-of-day line by staking out some place (how about Greenwich, England?) and reckoning time for all locations on the planet from that arbitrary starting place. (We probably would want to make allowances, of course, for certain geographical and political boundaries, even though that would tend to fuzz up the neat geometry of our meridians.)

But to really find out what time it is, in our experience and yours, some other matters also need to be considered.

Today is Saturday, hence part of a "weekend" (read "leisure time") rather than a "weekday" (read "workday"). That makes an enormous qualitative difference in *what* the day is.

Today is also near enough to a very special day—the 4th of July—to be a part of a very special weekend. In other years, when that special day lands on or close to a weekend, it generates what gets referred to as a "long weekend" (which, to quote Asimov, "is a period celebrated by automobile accidents").

But today has other meanings for us, and for you, meanings that derive from its temporal "location" in relation to certain recent, ongoing, or anticipated events, activities, or projects. For example, it is a day for us to celebrate because it marks the start of our work on the final revision of the manuscript for this book. It is a day of joyful anticipation for one of us because a good friend is due to visit tomorrow, and a day of joyful remembrance for the other because yesterday a manuscript was accepted for publication. It is a day of dread for one of us because next Monday—holiday notwithstanding—holds two unpleasant but unavoidable tasks. It is a day of dread for the other because the weather is expected to reach the 90s and the office air conditioning is ineffective. Without either glamorizing or trivializing these matters further, we can sum up succinctly by saying that *what time is it* is a complex question, indeed, and there are a multitude of answers to it.

Indeed, we live in many "times." We can place any given instant in many time frames. Some of those time frames are times to which we wish to give universal status: the official calendar, the official clock time, the "accepted" scientific statement of the age of the universe and the species (even here, of course, the universal status of many of these time frames is clouded by controversy). Some of these time frames are times to which we ascribe important, but strictly personal, meanings (today may be my birthday, but under most circumstances that is of no concern to you). Some of these time frames are times whose meanings derive from some specific situation or set of circumstances, or are times as reckoned "internal" to some organization, community, or behavior setting. These have neither universal nor personal meanings (the "2-minute warning" comes in the last 2 minutes of each half of every NFL football game, without regard to me or you or the prime meridian). Nevertheless, they affect our lives, insofar as we are touched by those organizations, communities, or behavior settings.

MULTIPLE TEMPORAL CONCEPTIONS
FROM THE INDIVIDUAL'S PERSPECTIVE

An individual in any culture lives his or her life within several embedding systems, each of which imposes somewhat different temporal conceptions on events. As we might expect, these actual *in situ* temporal conceptions are often much more mixed conceptions than the pure temporal paradigms discussed in the preceding chapter. These *in situ* time conceptions are mixed cases of the pure forms in two senses. First, they are mixed in the sense that they contain elements from two or more of the pure types we discussed in the preceding chapter. Second, they are mixed in the sense that, for some issue clusters, a given time perspective may actually contain dual positions— for example, that time is both unidirectional linear and cyclical.

Let us first note that in our culture—but by no means in all cultures—there is an *abstract* or *mathematical* time frame, and it has a central place in cultural concerns. That time frame follows *a strictly Newtonian conception*: In that abstract conception, time is viewed as divisible, homogeneous, hence a series of successions of instants; it is regarded as *reversible* as well as uniform in its passage, hence bidirectional–linear; it is treated as abstract and absolute (i.e., existing independent of objects and events) hence a time that is objective in a mathematical sense; and it is considered singular and measurable as a distinct dimension separate from other dimensions of existence (such as space, motion). There probably are many cultures in which there is no such abstract conception of time apart from time in relation to the physical and biological systems of the universe. But there is such a conception of time in our culture, the Newtonian conception, and it plays a dominant role in the life of the members of that culture.

Every culture has some conception of the physical universe in the concrete, whether or not it has an abstract mathematical conception; and these contain implicit temporal conceptions as well. In our culture, there is a time conception that we will call "geologic" time, already noted in the preceding chapter. It departs from the Newtonian in a number of respects. Although geologic time is a succession of divisible and homogeneous instants, as is Newtonian time, geologic time is *irreversible* and uniform in passage, hence unidirectional–linear. Furthermore, geologic time is absolute but concrete—considered to have real effects on objects—hence an *objective* time in a concrete or geological sense. Finally, geologic time is regarded as singular in principle, but it also considers that time is not necessarily a clearly differentiated dimension but rather is confounded with other dimensions of physical existence (hence it carries some aspects of the unified space–time continuum of the temporal paradigm of the "new physics").

Every culture also contains a conception of living systems and their development, with an implicit time conception that we will call "biologic" time. That biological conception of time departs even more sharply from the Newtonian conception and also differs from the geologic conception. Biologic time is, in fact, quite close to the *Transactional* temporal paradigm discussed in the preceding chapter. For the biologic conception, time is divisible but differentiated, hence epochal. It is irreversible but phasic in its passage, hence developmental (that is, it is characterized by spirals rather than recurrent cycles). It is relational rather than absolute, and is also concrete in its effects, hence experiential (rather than either geologic objective or mathematical objective). Biologic time involves multiple time concepts, although each is a distinct and separable dimension not necessarily confounded with other dimensions of phyical existence. Thus, biologic time differs from Newtonian time on six of the eight dimensions and from geologic time on five of the eight dimensions. It is in a different quadrant from both Newtonian time and geologic time for all four "clusters" of the temporal conceptions.

Any given culture must provide a value orientation schema that somehow "embraces" and makes sense of both the universe as a physical system and the universe as an ecology of living systems as well. Furthermore, it must do so in a way that permits its members to carry out both its technological or instrumental requirements and its social or interpersonal requirements. But a culture can do that in various ways and can provide a more or less effectively integrated schema. Our own culture does not offer its members a fully integrated set of value orientations. Some apply to its technological structures and some to its social structures, and these two subsets contain differing temporal conceptions.

In the main, our culture's construction of its technological requirements draws heavily upon the Newtonian temporal paradigm; but there are departures, and there are some "dual positions." We will call the dominant time conception of the culture's technological requirements "organizational time," because so much of the work of our culture gets done in the context of work organizations. (This time conception was also noted, briefly, in the preceding chapter, and listed in Table 2-1.) This conception views time as a succession of divisible and homogeneous instants, but with certain epochal features (seasons, work shifts, overtime, etc.). It views time mainly as having an irreversible and phasic flow (hence, developmental time) but also contains some aspects of a unidirectional linear conception. It views time as absolute and abstract, hence a mathematical time; and it views time as singular and independently measurable. Thus, it differs from all three of the time conceptions discussed thus far in this section on at least one of the four quadrants and on several of the dimensions.

Our culture's construction of its social or interpersonal requirements, on the other hand, draws its temporal conception largely from the Transactional paradigm discussed earlier, the paradigm underlying biologic time. In that view, time is epochal, developmental, experiential, and involves multiple independent time constructs. This time conception differs markedly from the one we have called organizational time.

The organism is thus faced with five or six embedding systems, each with its own temporal conception, some of them sharply differing from one another (see Figure 3-1). The individual must somehow deal with (we are tempted to say cope with) all of those conceptions with respect to each instant of

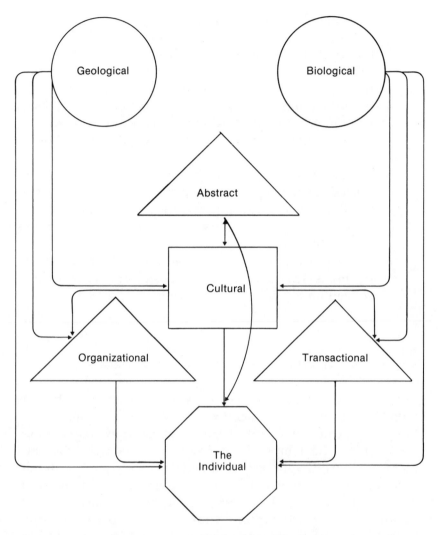

Figure 3-1. A cascade model of time frames.

time (or, perhaps more accurately, with respect to the time referents of every event). These several temporal conceptions are:

1. the individual as part of a physical universe, and the associated "geologic" conception of time;

2. the individual as part of an ecology of living systems, and the associated "biologic" conception of time;
3. the individual as a system of instrumental activities in relation to the culture's technological environment, and the associated "organizational" conception of time;
4. the individual as a system of interpersonal activities in relation to the culture's social structures, and the associated interactional or "Transactional" conception of time;
5. the individual as an autonomous member of the culture, a social-psychological entity, and the associated "cultural" conception of time (which may or may not successfully integrate various time conceptions for the individual); and
6. at least in our own culture, an abstract conception of the universe and its associated abstract ("Newtonian") conception of time.

RELATIONS AND CONFLICTS AMONG THE TIME FRAMES

People need, somehow, to reckon with differences in the various time frames with which they must deal. They may try to bring them into some sort of harmony. Or they may attempt to construct the temporal equivalent of logic-tight compartments: to live different parts of their lives in relation to different time conceptions, to march at different times to different drummers, so to speak. Graham (1981) suggests just such a temporal "multilingual" strategy. But if those time frames are based on sharply contrasting time conceptions, either harmony or segregation of activities can be difficult to bring about. Some examples may help make the point.

Consider our clock and calendar. The currently dominant ones, the Gregorian calendar and the 12- or 24-hour clock of 60-minute hours, are remarkably young in their status as a worldwide time system. It was not until early in this century, when postrevolutionary Russia adopted our most recent calendar corrections, that it could be said to have worldwide status, and even that statement reflects a strong Western culture bias.

The central and common unit for the clock and calendar is the day. A day is intended to reflect one rotation of the earth on its axis; but that rotation can be reckoned with respect to the sun, the moon, or the stars of our galaxy and those all constitute somewhat different lengths (Asimov, 1968). Furthermore, a year is intended to reflect one revolution of the earth around its orbit, but (1) that, too, can be reckoned with respect to the sun, the moon and/or the stars (a solar, lunar, or sidereal year, respectively), and, in any case, (2) the earth's passage around the sun is not some even number of 24-hour days. Our year is, in fact, *about* 365.25 days—but not exactly that value either (more exactly, the "tropical" year, the version of the solar year most tightly tied to earth seasons, is *approximately* 365.24220 days long). The month, originally intended to reflect one passage of the moon around the earth, is not divisible without remainder by a 24-hour day (it is *approximately* 29.5306 days), nor is it a submultiple without remainder of either a solar or a sidereal year (it is, of course, a submultiple of a lunar year—a 13-month year—but that year does not correspond to either a solar or a sidereal year).

As a consequence, we currently have a 12-month calendar with different numbers of days in various months. That calendar disregards phase of moon in relation to time of month (which in earlier times and other cultures was a prime consideration in formulating the calendar). Phase of moon rotates 13 times through 12 calendar months. Furthermore, in order to keep the seasons in close synchrony with the calendar (no trifle, for an agriculture-based society), by keeping constant the date on which the vernal equinox occurs, we correct our calendar by adding a full day once every 4 years (leap year), in those years whose A.D. number is divisible by 4. But that alone does not suffice to put our calendar in line with the heavens. We must add a further correction, by *omitting* leap year in every year that: (1) is divisible by 4, but (2) is also divisible by 100 (that is, every century), *unless* (3) that year also is divisible by 400 (that is, every 4 centuries), in which case we include the leap day in that year. (Hence we have 97 leap years in every 400 years). Even that highly makeshift set of adjustments does not actually put our calendar into perfect harmony with the heavens, but since the remaining discrepancies are so small that they are not noticeable within millennia (a matter of 0.12 days per 400 years, or nearly 3 hours in 400 years, or about 1 day in 3400 years), they can be, and currently are, ignored.

According to Asimov (1968), the need for these "leap" corrections was pointed out by Roger Bacon to Pope Urban IV in 1263, but was not acted on until 1582, by Pope Gregory XIII (hence, the name of our Gregorian calendar). By the late 16th century, however, the Protestant nations of Europe were not willing to follow the Pope's lead. None of them made the changes decreed by Gregory until 1700. England and its American colonies did not adopt those changes until 1752. Russia did not adopt them until post–World War I (but with an additional, still more accurate, adjustment). The Eastern Orthodox churches have still not accepted the Gregorian adjustments.

Why such a juryrigged calendar?

Because we are trying to impose a Newtonian time frame on a non-Newtonian galaxy!

There is *no* length of hour, no number of hours per day, no number of days per month, no number of days or months per year, that will, at one and the same time, preserve all of the complex temporal relations among earth, moon, sun, and stars, while providing humans on the planet Earth with a uniform number of hours, days, and months in a uniform year.

Newton's time involves homogeneous instants that are uniform in their passage. The galaxy involves time that is epochal (such as the vernal equinox, dawn, the new moon), and phasic in its passage (with the equinox, the dawn, and the new moon all coming back again and again). The hour is one 24th of a day (nearly!). Each hour is composed of 60 minutes; each minute has 60 seconds. These are arbitrary conventions carried over from earlier arithmetics and geometries, just as arbitrary as (but far less systematic than) the smaller scale units of milliseconds, nanoseconds, and the like. *None of these units of Newtonian time bear any tight linkage to the times required for axial rotations or orbital transits of any of the heavenly bodies.* Yet we persist in using them to calibrate the complex movements of that astronomical system.

The contradictions produced by the juxtaposition of time frames that draw from different temporal paradigms can be seen, as well, at the individual level. Consider the question of age, and its many subquestions about "how old is old enough" with respect to various human activities. If we look across history and cultures, we can see that these questions have had a wide range of answers for each of many types of human enterprise: Age at which one can (or should) learn to read, write, and cipher; age at which retirement from active work affairs is to be expected; age at which one can, or should, get married and conceive children; age to which one can reasonably expect to live, barring fatal accidents or special diseases; age at which one can become a warrior, a farmer, a chief or prince or politician; age at which one can make one's own decisions; and age at which one can safely be allowed to wield dangerous objects such as spears, guns, or automobiles. Many of these reflect the juxtaposition of features of the dominant cultural time frame for reckoning chronological age with features of either the technological (organizational) or the interactional (Transactional) time frames.

We reckon chronological age in terms compatible with Newtonian time, with certain roundings and approximations (such as age to the last birthday or age rounded to the nearest birthday) that reflect a more epochal form of time. Yet one's "age" in terms of career, for example, depends on the particular work role involved as well as on chronological age as such. Mathematicians, it is said, are over the hill by their middle 20s, an age when male baseball pitchers are just approaching their primes and female gymnasts are long past theirs. Furthermore, in work organizations, career time is more phasic in its passage, and more epochal in character, than the classical Newtonian conception on which chronological age is based.

The same sort of contrasts hold for the reckoning of time in familial and other social structures. For many years, our culture held strong norms that pushed women toward marriage and childbearing at much earlier ages than the norms applied to their male counterparts. This had far less to do with fertility and physiology than with social and economic circumstances. Those norms have changed markedly in recent years, reflecting new social and economic realities, not new physiological conditions. Still, the "proper" time for a woman to return to work following birth of a child is judged far more in relation to the age of her child(ren), and other social and economic matters, than in relation to age and health of the woman or time since delivery. Time, in social and familial roles, is not only epochal but also relational—relative to objects and events—and distinctly phasic in its passage.

The technological and social requirements of our culture are often addressed as if they are inherently in conflict with one another, and that conflict often is played out in terms of time. In our culture, the time demands of the work setting often seem to dominate the whole of the individual's life, swamping not only the time demands of social and family systems but also the time demands of the environment and the organism. So, certain times get *defined* in terms of their relation to time demands of the job ("stayed late at the office," "worked overtime"), while we ignore or suppress their simultaneous interpersonal meanings ("time to be home for dinner," or "game time for son's little league team," or even "must get some rest to shake this cold"). In its most extreme form, this "workaholic" stereotype suggests that time devoted to work is determined by the apparent needs of the organization and the stated or implied consequences for the individual's career; whereas time devoted to family (or to self as a biological or social-psychological entity) is established, residually, as time left over from the needs of work.

Furthermore, while from the point of view of the individual, a career is often seen as progressive, if not linear, from the point of view of the work organization careers are clearly recurrent cycles. Workers and supervisors come and go and younger ones replace them. Concepts like seniority probably have different meanings for the worker and the organization. In the Newtonian, unidirectional–linear time that the worker may apply to the concept, "senior" means added experience, hence added value. In the cyclical aspect of organizational time, "senior," may mean obsolete, worn, costly, ready to be replaced.

TEMPONOMICS: THE ECONOMIC METAPHOR

Doob (1971) did an analysis of adages about time, and found five main themes. The first three are: Time is precious, time is helpful, and time should be allocated wisely. (Incidentally, the other two are conflicting ideas about the relation of people and time: that time can and should be conquered and controlled; and that in the end time conquers all.) Lakoff and Johnson (1980) gathered metaphors involving time and organized most of them into three linked themes: Time is scarce, hence valuable, hence not to be wasted. Both of these analyses, and other sources of information regarding our cultural values about time, point to strong tendencies to interpret time within an economic metaphor.

Within that metaphor, the usual perspective treats time as a scarce resource that can be saved, earned, wasted, killed, and in general, used as a medium of exchange. Such a *temponomic view* is now so strongly entrenched in our culture that it may well be a crucial feature of the conceptual premises underlying modern-day work organizations. For example, the idea of time as a medium of exchange is fundamental not only to wages, schedules, and benefits (expressed in terms of sick-leave days and vacation days), but also to notions of productivity, seniority, and the like.

Given that view of time as an inherently scarce resource that can serve as a medium of exchange, it is a natural next step to ask about ways in which one can better manage one's scarce (and therefore valuable) time. There are a number of ways in which one can alleviate time conflicts (having two things scheduled for the same time) and resolve various other time management problems. These can be thought of as a "Waste-Time Recovery System" (see McGrath & Rotchford,

1983, for further discussion of such waste-time recovery techniques).

But time can be viewed in alternative ways as well, even within an economic metaphor. Time can be regarded, not as a scarce resource to be conserved and managed, but rather as a *fundamental dimension of social experience*. This view of time is perhaps more consistent with the way time is conceived of in modern physics than is the "scarcity" view just elaborated. In this view, time is regarded as one aspect of what must be "managed" in interpersonal affairs, in the same sense that the who, what, and where of social interaction must be managed (as in Altman's, 1975, work on privacy). In this view, time is like stimulation, space, social contact, and the like: In the *short run*, you can have either too much or too little of each of them. With too much, time weighs heavy on one's hands, and sometimes it has to be killed or wasted. With too little, time flies— and escapes. In that perspective, time is neither scarce nor abundant. Rather, it is *inexorable* in its passage. You can neither save it nor give it away; nor can you add to your allotted supply of it (you can, of course, "waste" time, but that is a matter of definition regarding the value of various time-filling activities).

If we treat time as a fundamental dimension of living, then what we need is not so much a waste-time recovery system but rather a time-investment handbook, a catalogue of ways to *use time to cope with other aspects of living*. In that regard, we might imagine highly "inefficient" uses of time that would be valuable toward some ends other than short-run task-performance efficiency (time as potlatch, you might say!). And we might imagine viewing not time but (psychological) energy as the scarce resource that needs to be conserved and managed (again fully in keeping with the "new physics"). Given that premise, we might well redefine certain seemingly "inefficient" uses of time (e.g., for vacations, for long walks, for regular and sufficient sleep) as highly productive—in an energy use-and-replenishment sense.

While such a perspective is inherent within the very temponomic view so prevalent within our culture, and, in fact, jibes better with a Transactional conception of time than does the "scarcity" version, very little work has been done from that kind of orientation, at least within the mainstream social science literature. To develop such a perspective parallel to the idea of a "waste-time recovery system" probably requires beginning with the premise that time is a dimension of living that passes inexorably. The aim might be to present a discussion (if not a catalog) of *ways in which available temporal resources can be invested to cope with life's other problems*—good ways to spend time or invest time, rather than good ways to save it. This is a view that might be called "supply side temponomics!"

Perhaps a useful way to talk about the difference between these two ways of construing time is in terms of *what* is being managed. In the former version, in which time is seen as a scarce resource, time is to be managed in the sense that one manages a budget or a flow of money. In the latter version, in which time is seen as a basic dimension of our experience, time is to be managed in the sense that one manages the flow of a river. The basic difference between them lies in the following contrast: Is time regarded as a more or less *automatically renewable but nonretainable resource*, as is the water flowing in a river? If so, then it can be "invested" or used but not saved. Alternatively, is time regarded as a resource whose *renewability is problematic and whose retainability is possible*, as is the money flowing through a business or a household? If so, then it can be saved and it may be spent but must not be wasted.

The central point, here, is that how people experience time in their lives is affected profoundly by the conceptions they have about that experience, and those conceptions in turn are influenced both by the dominant cultural preferences and by time conceptions arising from a number of variant conceptions. It is possible to *change the meaning of events* by changing the time conception with which those events are approached. A long walk is either "recreating" or loafing. A sabbatical leave can be viewed either as a boondoggle, or as an opportunity for growth and enhancement of future productivity—a capital investment, with time viewed as a form of capital. A planned dinner with a subordinate is either a necessary but pointless waste of time or the bestowing of status (by "giving" time to the relationship). While little work has been done directly regarding these conceptions, there may be considerable work that may bear on them, at least tangentially.

Some of the conflicts involving time, of course, have nothing to do with different time conceptions but rather have to do with inherent temporal scarcity, ambiguity, and conflict— matters that will be taken up in a later chapter of the book. But some of the conflicts involving time seem to arise because of, or at least be aggravated by, temporal matters that involve comparisons across time frames that are derived from different philosophical conceptions of time. Indeed, such conflict between temporal conceptions also underlies many of the problematic features of the substantial research literature on the psychological experience of time.

A BRIEF NOTE ON CULTURAL AND INDIVIDUAL DIFFERENCES IN TIME ORIENTATIONS

The treatment of time as a scarce and therefore valuable resource is a phenomenon quite characteristic of our culture, but it is by no means a cross-cultural universal. Indeed, there are wide differences among cultures in their overall orientations toward time. Not all cultures adopt the classical Newtonian conception. Nor do all give time such a central place in their cultural values as we do. But all cultures construe temporal phenomena in some way; and that conception of time affects how people in that culture experience and use time, just as our culture's conceptions of time affect behavior within it.

There has been some work on individual differences in temporal orientations. Cottle (1967) has done some excellent work that opens up interesting methodological possibilities in this area; so has Cohen (1964, 1966) and others. Regarding cross-cultural differences, Kluckhohn and Strodtbeck (1961) noted major cultural differences in value orientation patterns, including one temporal dimension (past, present, and future orientations). In a different line of inquiry, Jones (1980) has offered a five-part conception of ways in which people experience events: time, rhythm, improvisation, oral expression, and spirituality (TRIOS). Jones argues that the experience of blacks differs from the experience of members of the dominant (white, middle-class) cultural group in the United States, and that these differences (partly in time perspective) hinder communication and effective collective action.

Recently, there has been a minor surge of work on temporal orientations, some speculative and some empirical, some cross-cultural and some not. Graham (1981) identified three patterns that, he argues, characterize cultures at different technological levels. In the first, a "procedural–traditional" view, the amount of time spent on activities is irrelevant. Activities are procedure driven, not time driven. What is important is that things be done the right way, not that they be done on time, or at some given time, or in a minimum time. In the second pattern, a "circular–traditional" view, time is regarded as cyclical, epochal, holistic. Within that pattern, time is not regarded as divided into segments. There is the implication that we can do many things during the same time. Time is *there*, not "passing" or ticking away. It is not regarded as a scarce (hence valuable) resource. The third pattern, that Graham calls "linear–separable," he regards as the dominant pattern of our culture. Time is viewed as linear, abstract, homogeneous, and divisible. There is an implication that we can do only one thing at a time, and that time is to be regarded as a scarce, hence valuable, commodity.

Recently, both Gonzalez and Zimbardo (1985) and Levine and Wolff (1985) published articles on temporal orientations in the same issue of *Psychology Today*. The former proposed seven temporal perspectives derived from a factor analysis of responses to a magazine questionnaire. Levine and Wolff (1985) reported a cross-cultural comparison of the pace of life in large and medium sized cities in seven countries, based on earlier work by Levine and colleagues (Levine & Bartlett, 1984; Levine, West, & Reis, 1980). They argue that one can characterize a country (a culture) in terms of a unitary "pace of life" or social time that applies to many features of life in that land, from accuracy of clocks (and trains) to average walking speed and norms for promptness–lateness on a variety of social occasions.

All three of these characterizations of current U. S. culture—Graham's linear–separable pattern, Gonzalez and Zimbardo's dominant first factor that they label "future, work motivation–perseverence," and Levine and Wolff's relatively fast pace of social time in the U. S. cities—are in substantial correspondence with our description of the dominant temporal conception of our culture. Levine and Wolff's discussions of other cultures, particularly Indonesia, to some extent suggest features of Graham's other two orientations, procedural–traditional and circular–traditional, as does Jones's description of temporal features of TRIOS. Those, in turn, seem to embody elements of the Transactional paradigm and of the Eastern mystical as well. Gonzalez and Zimbardo's other six factors reflect various elements of the Newtonian, Transactional, and organizational time conceptions.

One valuable and innovative feature of Levine's work is the use of observational measures—walking speed, accuracy of bank clocks, speed of operation of the postal service—rather than just self-report measures (or simply speculations) to identify temporal orientations. The use of such objective indices of temporal orientations suggests that we could regard data on how people allocate their time among activities as evidence about their value orientations regarding time. Robinson and colleagues (e.g., Robinson & Converse, 1972) have done some landmark work here. This is one of the few questions in time research on which there is a solid and substantial data base. That data base needs updating, and expanding in terms of more detailed questions such as: How do people make time allocation decisions? How do they allocate time among activities within a day and over longer stretches of time? How do they allocate time among personal relationships? Across settings? Across roles?

These questions, of course, take the matter far beyond simply measuring (or inferring) temporal orientations. They raise fundamental questions about how people make use of their time to help cope with their various life tasks. This includes questions about how time is used as an interpersonal boundary-regulation mechanism, to control the flow of interpersonal interactions. Altman's (1975) work on privacy is germane here, but there is little other work that bears on these questions.

A proper appreciation of such cultural differences in temporal orientations and other temporal phenomena would require analysis of a vast and complex cross-cultural literature. We have neither space enough nor expertise to do that task adequately. Therefore we will not attempt to examine, systematically, such cross-cultural differences in temporal phenomena. Consequently, we feel obliged to remind readers that much of what we are presenting in this book is limited largely to more or less contemporary Western culture. That is a serious and substantial limit. But even within that limit, there remains a vast and complex area of inquiry, as evidenced in the material presented up to this point and as will be further shown in the chapters to follow.

In the next section, we will again turn to a conflict between time frames for the individual. We will examine the juxtaposition of Newtonian and Transactional time frames raised by questions in the psychophysics of time.

THE PSYCHOLOGICAL EXPERIENCE OF TIME

The one area in which there has been extensive research on time within the field of psychology deals with subjective judgments of the passage of time. Throughout this century, experimental psychologists have given considerable attention to, and conducted extensive empirical research on, the mapping between the objective passage of time and the individual's subjective experience of time. In large part, this work has been done in the tradition of classical psychophysics and has carried with it all of the assumptions of that area of study.

In particular, work on the psychophysics of time accepts, and is stated in terms of, a strict mind–body dualism. The psychophysics of vision distinguished between the reception of the physical energy of light (sensation) and the interpretation of that received energy as visual form and color (perception). The point of it was the attempt to adduce formal statements of how one of these is translated into the other. Similarly, the psychophysics of time distinguished between the "reception" of a period of elapsed time (construed as concrete and absolute, if not literally physical energy) and the "interpretation" of that received interval as a temporal duration. The point of it was the attempt to map those translations as formally as possible.

The psychophysics of time thus also accepts a second major assumption of the psychophysics approach: That in the mapping between two continua, one from the environment and one from within the individual, the former is to be regarded as "true" and the latter is to be calibrated to it. Those involved in the psychophysics of vision asked how (and perhaps why) humans "distorted" their sensory input to experience a pattern somewhat different from the stimulus input pattern. Similarly, those working on the psychophysics of time asked how (and why) people distorted "true" or objective time into somewhat different patterns of perceived time.

Findings from the psychophysics of time are voluminous, detailed, and yet incomplete and containing unresolved issues. Much of this material has been well summarized and interpreted by Doob (1971) in a very scholarly and readable book. Fraisse (1984) has provided a more recent review of parts of that work, so there is no need for detailed and extensive coverage of that work in this chapter. This section will therefore be limited to a brief summary of some of the main findings, a discussion of some of the main unresolved issues, and an attempt to tie this material in with the overall perspective of this book.

THE PSYCHOPHYSICS OF TIME

First, it should be pointed out that the classical psychophysical methods that are used in almost all work on the psychophysics of time involve highly artificial, laboratory-like experimental conditions (a research strategy that Runkel & McGrath, 1972, call "judgment studies"). Furthermore, although these methods subsume only a relatively narrow band of the methodological spectrum available to behavioral and social sciences (one of eight possible types of research strategy, according to Runkel & McGrath, 1972), results turn out to be very sensitive to differences among the methods within that narrow band (see Doob, 1971, for an extensive discussion of these method-based differences). So any statement of "findings" must take those methodological limitations into account.

Even with such a caveat, however, it is clear that the accumulated work on the psychophysics of time has made substantial progress in determining a number of key baseline values. Doob states a series of key questions that have been asked and (more or less) answered about the experience of time.

1. How long must an interval be to be perceived and reported? This is the problem of threshold.
   Answer: Slightly over 0.01 second for sound; between 0.07 and 0.10 second for light.
2. How long can an interval be and yet remain in the psychological present, perceived as a unified event? This is the problem of duration or temporal unity.
   Answer: From 2 to 12 seconds for simple stimuli.
3. What is the minimum separation interval needed for two stimuli to be perceived as separate entities? This is the problem of succession and is related to questions of rhythm.
   Answer: For perception of two entities, but not their order, 0.0001 second for noise, 0.0002 second for tones, and 0.16 second for visual flicker. For perception of their order, also, 0.02 second is needed for judgments that are correct 75% of the time, and that holds both for same modality judgments and for judgments of stimuli involving two different modalities or sense organs.
4. What is the optimal duration for accurate judgments of duration of (very short) intervals? This is the problem of the indifference point or indifference zone. It springs in part from typical findings that short intervals are overestimated and long ones are underestimated.
   Answer: About 0.50 second to 0.75 second.

5. How big must the difference in duration between two intervals be before they can be accurately judged as of different durations? This is the problem of the application of Weber's law to time judgments.
   Answer: Perhaps 10%, but the matter of the strict applicability of Weber's law is still controversial.
6. How are objective and subjective time related?
   Answer: Probably in the form of a family of power functions, with a different constant exponent for each individual (but the evidence for this is relatively weak and scattered).

Note that this work attacks one of the basic philosophical issues discussed earlier: the relation between objective and subjective time. Virtually all of it is done on the assumptions that time is divisible but homogeneous, uniform in passage, abstract and absolute, and singular and measurable. Moreover, the singular and measurable time that is valid is the objective time derived from the outside clock; and any differences between that time and experienced time are to be regarded as some kind of "error" on the part of the individual. Thus, this work is based on a Newtonian conception of time (with the exception that it does not permit a reversible time). That is to say, it buys the dominant cultural conception of time.

Moreover, like other portions of psychophysics (and of experimental psychology), this work draws on physical sciences rather than biological sciences for its conceptual models as well as its methods. Very little of the work, for example, takes into account *time of day* at which the judgments are elicited. But the evidence from analysis of temperature, activity, and other cycles makes it clear that *all* judgments, but especially temporal judgments, are likely to vary depending upon the point within the individual's circadian activity cycles at which they are taken.

There is, of course, much more that needs to be said, at a much more detailed level, for a full appreciation of this body of work. That task will not be undertaken here, since there are several good presentations of that work, already cited. Instead, we will consider, briefly, the contributions of two other bodies of work done from the perspective of other fields of psychology (human factors and clinical, respectively) to the study of the same problems. Then we will try to formulate a model of one of the remaining major issues in this area: how judgments of passage of time are affected by the content of events occurring during the interval, and by the condition of the organism.

OTHER FACTORS AFFECTING JUDGMENTS OF TIME

There are two other substantial bodies of empirical research on time at the psychological level. One is out of the tradition of human factors (or human engineering) psychology. The other is out of the tradition of clinical psychology. Both of these bodies of literature constitute attempts to search for factors that affect time judgments. In a sense, they each take the psychophysics work as the normative case and explore what intra-individual and situational factors further modify those baseline relations.

The human factors work emphasizes the behavior of normal individuals, who may vary in attitudes, abilities, and the like, and who may perform tasks under situational conditions that vary in such factors as task difficulty, environmental constraints, and so forth. The clinical approach emphasizes the abnormal, both intra-individual and situational abnormalities. For example, this approach would include the study of effects on time judgments of such abnormalities as psychoses, drugs, tumors or other pathologies, and hypnotic states. But the two approaches are alike in accepting the psychophysics approach and its results as establishing the "true" time baseline for correcting subjective time so that it is in accord with objective time. In this view, their own work can be regarded as studying how various factors (be they task difficulty or use of a psychotropic drug) further decrease the accuracy of time judgments, requiring still further corrections. Hence, they also share the tendencies of psychophysics to treat time as abstract and absolute, uniform in passage, and generally in accord with the Newtonian conception.

Many personal and situational factors, both normal and abnormal, that have effects on task performances in general also tend to have effects on the performance of the task involved in making judgments of the passage of time. Much of these two rather substantial bodies of literature is well summarized by Doob and others and will not be examined in detail here. The relevant factors are many and complex, and the findings seem to involve at least some contradictions. We will summarize the main findings, in the context of trying to formulate a model of these judgments, after a brief discussion of some other such models.

INTERNAL CLOCKS AND INFORMATION PROCESSING

The idea of an internal biological or psychological clock has long been considered by researchers in these areas but remains controversial. When some of the early studies of time estimates (e.g., Hoagland, 1935) found them to vary with body temperature and with administration of certain drugs, it was postulated that the speed of time units as we perceive them might be controlled by body temperature, which in turn depends on the body's chemical activity. (In spite of this relation, the clearly cyclical pattern of body temperature seems not to have been taken into account either in arguments about the biological clock or in research on judgments of the passage of time.)

There were many attempts to relate subjective experience of time to various biological processes such as heart rate, respiration rate, cellular metabolism, and brain processes (see Hamner, 1966, for a review). But none of these seemed to map, uniquely, to time estimation. Hence, some workers in this area apparently concluded that, since no specific location for a biological clock had been found, such a clock did not exist (see Ornstein, 1969, for an explicit presentation of such an argument, in a book that presents an alternative model of these processes that does not assume an internal clock). In contrast, at least one prominent biologist (Pittendrigh, 1972), argues that there are a multiplicity of biological clocks, not just one, and that their synchronization—mutual entrainment—is the central problem in understanding the organization of the biological organism as a system.

By the early 1960s, several investigators had proposed information-processing models that described the experience of time as a short-term memory phenomenon (Fraisse, 1963; Frankenhaeuser, 1959). Their basic premise was that the duration of experienced time depends on how much information registers in short-term memory during the target interval. Specifically, the subjective duration of an interval lengthens as more information is put into the short-term memory register. Such a model could account for many of the empirical findings in this area, including the lengthening of time experienced with the administration of various stimulant drugs (e.g., Fischer, 1966), and the shortening of time experienced during empty intervals. But it cannot account for other replicated findings, including the reversal of some of these for judgments of time in passing versus judgments of the duration of past time intervals.

Ornstein's (1969) model, referred to above, is an information-processing model based on size of the regions in long-term memory in which information is stored. Judgments of duration of past intervals lengthen as the amount of information "stored" in long-term memory increases. In a series of nine studies, Ornstein showed that stimulus complexity, inefficient encoding, and increasing amounts of information in memory—all of which would be presumed to increase the "size" of the long-term memory storage region devoted to that material—all significantly lengthened the subjective experience of time.

But the subjective experience of time is both a short-term memory and a long-term memory phenomenon, depending on whether you are referring to judgments of time in passing or judgments of times past. The earlier information-processing models dealt with the former; Ornstein's deals with the latter. We agree with Doob's interpretation, that a psychological clock or some near equivalent is needed to account for *both* judgments of time in passing and judgments of times past. Ornstein's model simply does not account for judgments of time in passing. The earlier short-term memory models did not account for judgments of time in the past.

Recent research on biological rhythms apparently points to the existence of at least two loosely and asymetrically coupled timing mechanisms, and offers evidence regarding the location of one of them (Moore-Ede *et al.*, 1982). But in any case, we believe that whether or not researchers have yet identified—or ever will identify—a "location" for such a "clock" (or clocks) has little to do with the usefulness of such a concept in a model of these judgment processes. Finally, we agree with Pittendrigh that our central concern ought to be with identifying the processes by which the multiple internal "clocks" become synchronized, mutually entrained to one another, and what the consequences are of disruptions of such synchronizations.

A MODEL OF TIME JUDGMENTS

To some extent, specific findings in this area can be summarized around three main issues (again following Doob):

1. Differences in judgments of duration of time intervals in passing versus judgments of length of time intervals that occurred in the past.
2. Effect on those time judgments of factors that tend to increase, versus factors that tend to decrease, the rate of external stimulation during the interval being judged.
3. Effects on those time judgments of factors that tend to increase, versus factors that tend to decrease, the individual's internal state of excitation or arousal.

While the summary to follow suggests more unanimity of results than a strictly accurate detailed review of the literature would offer (see Doob's, 1971, excellent review of these differences), it is an attempt to interpret what is clearly the dominant *pattern* of findings in a fairly straightforward way.

In describing these effects, it is useful to make two assumptions. One is that there is some kind of "standard" or "expected" stimulus rate, probably one that varies with situations and is subject to adaptation; and that departures from that rate are noticed by the individual as "many" or "few" stimuli. The other assumption is that the organism has some kind of internal clock. We are conceiving of this clock as some kind of internalized memory, knowledge, or awareness of the passage of time. It need be no more complex than a resettable *counter*.

Stimulus-enriched intervals seem to pass faster than intervals with little stimulation in them. That is, intervals during which there is more stimulation than "usual" are experienced as shorter than relatively empty intervals (hence, the expression "time flies when you are having fun!"). But such "busy" intervals are *remembered* as if they were longer, while empty intervals are remembered as if they were shorter, than they "actually" were (as measured by objective clock time).

On the other hand, when changes in rate of apparent passage of time are produced by increasing or decreasing arousal levels (e.g., by drugs that increase excitation or tranquilize), then the effects seem to be opposite to those noted above. It is as if drugs and other conditions altered the operation of some kind of internal clock (or counter)—speeding it or slowing it in relation to the "outside" clock (which the experimenter is using to decide whether the subject's judgment of amount of time passed is an overestimate or an underestimate). Increasing the rate of metabolism, and in general increasing the level of excitation, seems to increase the rate of "ticking," so to speak, of an internal clock, and hence make it run *faster* than the "outside" clock, leading to a time judgment that is an overestimate of how much "outside" time has passed.

So, a person who has received stimulant drugs or is otherwise aroused, and so has an increased internal rate, will think that a short time interval is lasting a long time (though later recall may be the reverse). But a person subjected to a high stimulus rate (as before, a "stimulus-filled" interval) will judge a long interval as lasting only a short time (although memory will reverse that decision about duration if the individual is asked about it later). Presumably, this latter case is one in which the rate of "ticking" of the internal clock has not been quickened, but the rate of stimulus input from the external world has been increased beyond the normal or expected rate. Since more has happened during t seconds on the actual clock than usually happens in t seconds, *in memory* that interval is judged as if more than t seconds must have passed (time estimate is greater than t). But *in passing*, since there was very little time to handle the stimulus input that occurred, that interval must be short. Conversely, in a stimulus-impoverished interval, there were few stimuli involved and, therefore, little to remember; hence, it is remembered as if it was a short interval; but, in passing, there was so much time to "savor" each stimulus that there must have been a lot of time.

Another way to formulate these ideas is to consider the judgment of an interval, i, in passing (PTi) as being the product of the "objective" time of the interval on the clock (CTi), and two ratios: the ratio of beats of an internal clock to a "normal" clock rate (ITi/ITn); and the ratio of the normal number of stimuli per interval to the actual number of stimuli occurring during the interval in question (Sn/Si):

$$(PTi) = (CTi)\,(ITi/ITn)\,(Sn/Si)$$

On the other hand, the judgment or *recall* of a past interval (RTi) can be considered as the product of the "objective" time, (CTi) and the same two ratios, now both inverted: the ratio of number of stimuli to a standard that reflects the "normal" stimulus rate (Si/Sn); and the ratio of the normal internal clock rate to the ongoing internal clock rate (ITn/ITi):

$$(RTi) = (CTi)\,(Si/Sn)\,(ITn/ITi)$$

Furthermore, if we wish to make the assumption that under normal conditions, $ITn = Sn$—that is, that our expectations about a normal rate of stimulation is based on the normal "ticking" of an internal clock—then both of those terms drop out of both of the formulas, and we have:

$$(PTi) = (CTi) (ITi/Si) \quad \text{and}$$
$$(RTi) = (CTi) (Si/ITi) = (CTi) (Si/ITn)$$

Given this formulation, we would expect excitatory drugs or other conditions that increase arousal, or the metabolic rate, to increase ITi and thereby affect judgments of time in passing (PTi) during the time of that increased rate; but the internal clock would presumably be operating at a "normal" rate at a later time when the individual is asked to recall, and thus RTi judgments would be made against a "standard" ITi (or, more accurately, against a ratio of ITn/ITi equal to 1.00). Such increases in ITi should increase PTi (they make passing intervals seem longer) but have no effect on RTi judgments (assuming that the time intervals are being remembered while the organism is operating under "normal" internal states). Inhibitory drugs or other conditions that slow metabolic functions do the reverse.

On the other hand, enhancing the rate of external stimulation increases Si relative to Sn. This *decreases PTi* (it makes the passing interval seem shorter), but *increases RTi* (it makes remembered time intervals seem longer) because RTi judgments are made, presumably, on the basis of the amount of stimulation from that interval that is "stored" in long-term memory compared against a "standard" amount of stimulation per time. (This assumes that a certain amount of stimulus information in storage implies a certain amount of stimulus-processing time).

CONCLUDING COMMENTS

Our culture and many of the behavior settings within it put considerable emphasis on timeliness, timing, being on time, and having a keen sense of the passage of time. Distortions of such estimates of time passage can have negative consequences for the individual. For example, highly anxious people often see time as passing more quickly than it actually does. This added pressure may detract from the effectiveness of their performance. Individuals who score high on Type A personality measures often exhibit excessive responsiveness to time pressure, and the Type A pattern seems to be accompanied by a number of potential health risks.

However, we are impressed by how accurately humans can make time estimates, both with regard to time in passing and with regard to times past. We consider this as evidence that people become strongly entrained to the objective clock time of their surroundings. Research by Schachter and colleagues on the effects of "rigged" clocks on the eating habits of individuals (Schachter & Gross, 1968) suggests that such entrainment is pervasive and relatively malleable. That too would be in accord with the findings summarized here on judgments of duration of time intervals. It is to the subject of entrainment that we will now turn.

The Rhythms of Social Behavior

ENTRAINMENT IN GROUP INTERACTION AND TASK PERFORMANCE

In previous chapters, we have described several different ways in which time can be construed, and discussed how temporal factors permeate both our lives and our logic. In this chapter, we will propose a temporal framework that uses the idea of social entrainment as the central concept. That framework, we believe, may help us to understand and integrate many aspects of human behavior; it has served as a guide for most of the empirical work in our research program.

ENTRAINMENT

The entrainment framework uses a conception of time that is prominent within the biological sciences. It is, largely, the conception we called "transactional time" earlier in the book. In that view, time is divisible, but differentiated, and therefore epochal; irreversible and phasic in passage, and therefore developmental in its flow; relational and concrete, and therefore experiential; and composed of multiple time constructs, with no necessary convergence among them but with high differentiation between them and other concepts. The social entrainment model focuses especially on the phasic or developmental aspects of time.

The basis for the social entrainment model lies in the notion of entrainment as used in the biological sciences, in which one cyclic process becomes captured by, and set to oscillate in rhythm with, another process. Consider the problem of jet lag. A number of physiological processes, such as temperature and activity cycles, become coupled to each other and to the 24-hour clock. When a person travels across several time zones, these processes are no longer synchronized with the new clock time. This de-synchronization has a number of negative consequences, and those consequences continue until the cycles become re-entrained to one another and to clock time.

The social entrainment model proposes that this kind of entrainment can occur at psychological and social levels as well as at the physiological level. Numerous physiological, psychological, and behavioral cycles have been identified in humans. Furthermore, those cycles can become entrained to or modified by powerful social and environmental cues. The social entrainment model provides a framework for describing the operation of such endogenous, rhythmic processes, their coupling to one another and potentially to outside pacers, and the temporal patterns of behavior resulting from those rhythms of human behavior.

A PHYSIOLOGICAL EXAMPLE

The entrainment model is built upon evidence from the study of biological processes and can be explained best by means of a physiological example. There is clear evidence in the biological sciences for the operation of entrainment in different cyclical processes in the body. For example, in humans both skin and core body temperatures are cyclical, and so is activity or arousal level. The levels or rates of flow of many constituents of blood and urine also show such cyclical patterns in the same general temporal range (that is, circadian). These are endogenous cycles; that is, they are inherent in the life processes of the organism, and they occur whether or not they are in synchrony with the cycles of other processes, and whether or not they are being influenced by an outside pacer. These multiple endogenous rhythms represent the first part of the entrainment model.

There is a strong tendency for synchrony among such physiological cycles; that is, sets of such endogenous cycles tend to fluctuate together, in phase and periodicity. The idea of synchrony is more complex that it at first appears to be. It involves the idea of simultaneity (but, as we will point out in a later chapter, definitions of simultaneity always involve some degree of arbitrariness). Definitions of synchronization usually include at least two requirements: that there be a systematic relation between the periods of the (two or more) cycles whose synchronization is being explored; and that there be a systematic relation between the phases (i.e., time of onset or offset or both) of the cycles being examined. The periods can be identical, or they can be multiples of one another (e.g., harmonics). The phases can be in any systematic relation to one another, but the most common ones dealt with in studies of entrainment are in-phase (cycles are at their high points at the same time) and opposite phase (one cycle is at peak when the other is at low point).

Furthermore, although we are using the terms "cycles," "rhythm," and "oscillation" more or less interchangeably here, such endogenous temporal processes need not be smooth sine/cosine waves, nor smooth waves of any sort. At root, we are talking about *oscillations*. Such oscillations can be represented in many forms—smooth or complex wave patterns, step functions, sawtoothed or box-form waves, or simply patterns of on–off changes in state over time. What makes such a process a rhythm or cycle is not the smoothness or regularity of the pattern it traces during any one cycle, or oscillation, but the temporal regularity with which that pattern repeats.

When two such oscillations or cyclic processes, initially independent, become synchronized (as defined above), such coordination of phase and period is called "entrainment." For example, human temperature and activity level variations—oscillations, cycles, rhythms—are normally entrained to one another, such that when temperature is at its peak so is activity. There is considerable evidence, for humans and other animals, that many physiological and behavioral patterns can reasonably be regarded as autonomous rhythms that normally operate in such a state of mutual entrainment with one another.

There appears to be some evidence that these processes cluster into two groups. Moore-Ede, Sulzman, and Fuller (1982) call them system X and system Y. There is strong mutual entrainment among the components within each cluster and a somewhat weaker, and certainly more complex, coupling between the two systems. System X seems to be organized around core body temperature and rapid-eye-movement (REM) sleep, and to include several other metabolic and physiological processes; system Y seems to be organized around the rest–activity cycle, and to include skin temperature and slow-wave sleep, as well as several other metabolic and physiological processes. System Y seems clearly to be located in the superchiasmic nuclei (SCN); system X clearly not to be located in that region of the brain. System X and system Y are interdependent, but the coupling is both loose and asymmetrical: System X affects system Y far more than the reverse (Moore-Ede et al., 1982, estimate a 4 to 1 ratio of those effects). At the same time, it is through system Y that most environmental pacers seem to have their primary effects. System X and system Y—or whatever variations of such concepts eventually come to be accepted by biological scientists as the most useful concepts for these phenomena—appear to be two loosely and asymmetrically coupled synchronization systems. They seem to serve the purpose of a biological clock, at least at the level of circadian temporal patterns. Such synchronization system(s) are a second component of our social entrainment model.

Such mutual entrainment among endogenous patterns of oscillations yields observable behaviors that are temporally patterned. For example, alertness, hence performance on signal detection and problem-solving tasks, varies as a function of the phase—as well as the amplitude—of the temperature and activity cycles (that is, the phase and amplitude status of the normally synchronized systems X and Y). Alertness is at its peak when the entrained temperature–activity rhythms are at their peak. Thus, mental alertness follows a cyclic pattern during a day. (In terms of earlier discussion, this example illustrates how one minute is not like all other minutes. For the physiological and behavioral functioning of the organism, time seems to be phasic and epochal, Transactional rather than Newtonian.) Such temporal patterns of behavior constitute the third component of our social entrainment model.

External events or processes may operate to disturb—and re-entrain—one or more such clusters of mutually entrained cycles. Suppose, for example, that a scheduling change (e.g., going on night shift) causes a change in the activity–rest cycles of a particular person, such that he or she needs the highest levels of activity (and alertness) when the temperature cycle is at its low point. If such an external event is strong enough, the temperature and activity–rest cycles become de-synchronized or uncoupled from one another–disentrained–and the temporal patterning of behaviors related to those cycles (e.g., alertness and problem solving) become disrupted. Such disruption of patterns will persist until there is a re-entrainment of the cycles of the processes that underlie these patterns of behavior. Such external cycles or signals, that function as "pacers" or *zeitgebers* to de-synchronize and re-entrain temporal patterns, constitute the final component of our social entrainment model.

We will now describe how psychological and social processes can be construed as operating in these patterns of entrainment.

THE SOCIAL ENTRAINMENT MODEL

The Social Entrainment Model rests on five key propositions:

1. That much of human behavior, at physiological, psychological, and interpersonal levels, is temporal in char-

acter; that is, that the behavior is regulated by processes that are cyclical, oscillatory, or rhythmical.

2. That these are endogenous rhythms; that is, that they are inherent in the life processes of the organisms involved.
3. That sets of such rhythms, within the individual, become mutually entrained to one another, hence that they come to act in synchrony in both phase and frequency or periodicity.
4. That the temporal patterns of individuals who are in interaction become mutually entrained to one another, that is, that they get in synchrony of phase and period.
5. That temporal patterns of behavior of individuals and sets of individuals become collectively entrained to certain powerful external pacer events and entraining cycles. The former alter the phase or onset, and the latter alter the periodicity, of those endogenous and mutually entrained rhythms.

There is ample empirical evidence to support these propositions. Entrainment processes are pervasive in much of human behavior, including: motor activity patterns, sleep–wake cycles, reactions to changes in work schedules, activity patterns during work, vacation and holiday periods, temporal features of interpersonal interaction, and many more. By these strong assumptions, we are asserting the *generality* of such rhythms and of their entrainment. Specifically, we are asserting that various temporal rhythms underlie a wide range of social behavior and that synchronizations among them (or the lack of such synchronizations) have widespread and crucial implications for human cognition, social interaction, task performance, and role behavior, and therefore for human health and well-being.

The set of propositions listed above can also be expressed in the form of a four-component model (shown in Figure 4-1). The first component is a set of *multiple endogenous temporal/ rhythmic processes (RHYTHM)*. There are a host of such rhythms, ranging in their periodicities from years to fractions of a second. These include time-based processes that have to do with

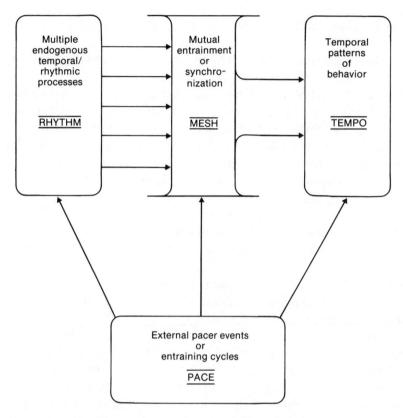

Figure 4-1. The social entrainment model.

life span development (birth, maturation, puberty, etc.); infradian cycles (such as monthly menstruation), a host of circadian cycles (temperature, activity, and various metabolic processes), and a number of ultradian rhythms (work–rest, respiration, endocrine secretion, etc.) that range in their periodicities from about 90 minutes (for activity cycles) down to a few seconds or fractions of a second (for some neural, vascular, and metabolic processes). While many of the examples listed are primarily physiological, some of them are also partly behavioral— the ultradian work–rest cycles, for example, and the fulfillment of the stages in the life span developmental cycles. Furthermore, many other behavioral patterns not listed (e.g., patterns of vocalizations and silences) also exhibit strong rhythmic qualities. (RHYTHM is our term for this component of the model.)

The second component of the model is some (postulated) *mutual entrainment, or synchronization, system (MESH)*. It is clear that, under what might be regarded as "normal" operating conditions, individual humans have all of their endogenous rhythms in synchrony. It is also clear that when such synchrony is disrupted (e.g., by flying west to east across several time zones), not only are those rhythms all put out of phase with an external time (time on the ground, so to speak), but they also are put (or soon become) out of synchronization with one another. Moreover, left alone over time, they will also become once again synchronized—that is, they will once again become mutually entrained. We therefore posit some system(s) or process(es)—some regulating device(s)—for the establishment and maintenance of such mutual entrainment of these multiple endogenous rhythms. (MESH is our term for this second component of the model.)

The third component of the model consists of the *temporal patterns expressed in the actual behaviors (TEMPO)* that are the subject of our attention. These include, for example, the time course of the actual growth and development of the organism; the actual temporal flow of activity and rest of some individual on some particular day; the temporal pattern of both core body temperature and skin temperature, high and low; the temporal flow of vocalizations and silences in some individuals' conversation; and many others. (We will use the term TEMPO for this third component of the model.)

In Figure 4-1, we show these three components as if they were linked in a linear chain, although there undoubtedly are numerous feedback loops operating as well. The many separate processes giving rise to the multiple endogenous rhythms (RHYTHM) become synchronized into one, or a few, mutual entrainment systems (MESH), which in turn yield a number of observable temporal patterns of behavior (TEMPO) that are in synchronization with one another (albeit often in complex synchronization patterns). The fourth component of the model lies outside of this causal chain, and potentially has an impact on each of the other three components. That fourth component is the set of all of those *external pacing events and entraining cycles* (*PACE*) that can affect those temporal patterns, either by triggering them (that is, by altering their onset or phase) or by "capturing" and modifying their periodicity. (We will use the term PACE for this fourth component of the model.)

An example of entrainment in a simple set of social behaviors may help clarify the components of the Social Entrainment Model. Consider two individuals, A and B, in conversation. Each of them enters the conversation with particular endogenous temporal patterns (RHYTHMs) that determine that person's individual (implicit) preferences for conversational patterns. These include such things as the individual's momentary position on an activity–rest cycle, as well as various psychological traits, needs, and states (e.g., intimacy and privacy needs, mood).

For an actual conversation to take place, the two people must somehow coordinate (MESH) their individual conversational patterns. This will come about partly via social conventions about appropriate conversational behavior (e.g., implicit rules or norms about turn-taking, sharing of floor time, appropriate length of turns and of silences, overall activity, and so forth). These norms are also influenced by the existing relationship between the two conversants—are they old friends, teacher–pupil, boss–employee, strangers?

The result of this coordination is a particular temporal pattern of conversational behavior for the two individuals (TEMPO). That is, the conversation itself will turn out to exhibit a fairly stable pattern of turn-taking, sound and silences, patterns of verbal and nonverbal content, that is the conversational pattern for this dyad on this occasion.

The fourth component of the model, PACE, refers to the occurrence of an external event that disrupts the established pattern of conversation. Suppose, for example, that the dyad notices some event in their surroundings, and their conversation shifts to a topic about which person A is a recognized expert. This is likely to alter the established pattern of their conversation. Speaking versus listening time is likely to be redistributed (so that the expert, A, talks relatively more). The pattern of content of the conversation is likely to shift (B will ask more questions, A will offer more answers or opinions). The pattern of nonverbal behavior is likely to shift (B, now listening more, will also spend more time looking at A). This new temporal pattern is likely to persist until the dyad ends its conversation, or is again disrupted by a new external event.

We will now turn to an examination of some evidence for the operation of the four components of the Social Entrainment Model in human behavior.

RHYTHM: DETECTING ENDOGENOUS CYCLICALITY

The advent of powerful mathematical and statistical tools for detecting temporal patterns, such as Fourier, spectral, and cross-spectral analyses, has made it possible for researchers to identify many rhythmic patterns in human behavior. For example, cycles with periods of approximately 90 minutes have been found for basic activity–rest patterns, REM sleep, oral activity, the ebb and flow of adrenocortical hormones, and aspects of cognitive style (Klein & Armitage, 1979; Luce, 1971). Consistent individual differences in cycle periodicity have been found for the proportion of time spent talking (Jaffe & Feldstein, 1970; Warner, Kenny, Stoto, 1979); amount of spontaneous psychomotor activity (Takala, 1975); body temperature and heart rate (Hoagland, 1935); speed of oral reading (Lass & Lutz, 1975); arm swinging tempo (Smoll, 1975); and a host of expressive behaviors such as walking, drawing, writing, and tapping (Allport & Vernon, 1933).

Temporal patterns in human interaction are of special interest in this regard. Systematic cycles have been detected in gaze and body movements during social interaction (Chapple, 1970). Cobbs (1973) and Warner (1979) have identified regular cycle lengths in conversations among college student dyads. Dabbs (1983) has detected systematic patterns that he calls "megaturns" in conversations dealing with cognitively difficult material. A megaturn is a period of high (but not totally uninterrupted) vocal activity by a particular participant, followed by a period of low (but not totally silent) vocal activity by that participant and a corresponding period of high vocal activity by another participant. Furthermore, while the speech and silence patterns of dyads are strongly entrained in an *opposite phase* pattern within a given conversational period, the overall speech and silence patterns of dyads are entrained in an *in-phase* pattern for longer periods of time (for example, over the course of a day). That is, when two people carry on a conversation, during a very large percentage of the time of that conversation, one of them is talking while the other is listening. But when we look at the interaction of two people over the course of a day, there is a strong tendency for the two of them to have their periods of high vocal activity (and of low activity) at the same time.

MESH: MUTUAL ENTRAINMENT OF ENDOGENOUS CYCLES

The evidence for mutual entrainment among physiological cycles is very strong. Most researchers in what has come to be called "chronobiology" now seem in agreement that cycles and rhythms, and therefore dynamic equilibrium, are fundamental organizational principles within biological systems. Rhythm helps to coordinate internal events (Goodwin, 1970). In fact, Pittendrigh (1972) argues that an organism can be depicted as a loosely coupled population of oscillators, and that understanding these dynamic coupling processes is the central problem for understanding the organization of biological systems. The same reasoning has been applied to social systems by Chapple (1970) and Iberall and McCulloch (1969). Rhythm reflects the underlying dynamic equilibrium processes by which the many aspects of complex social systems are coordinated. Both Strauss (1965) and Warner (1984) argue that each person brings into a social system a set of (implicit) preferences about such matters as activity rates, time allocations, and the like. During a period of social interaction, the members of that social system must work out a "negotiated temporal order" in which they adjust their activity patterns to coordinate with one another. Each member of the social system can be viewed as an oscillator (or as a set of loosely coupled and mutually entrained oscillators); that is, the person's activity will show one or more patterns of alternation over time. Just as with physiological processes, these oscillatory patterns of the members become *coupled*, or coordinated, or *mutually entrained*, with those of other members of the social system (Warner, 1984). The multiple independent cycles of activity of the members of a social system become coordinated with one another into a temporally patterned system of activity that is characterized by a dynamic equilibrium rather than by a fixed homeostatic pattern.

TEMPO: TEMPORAL PATTERNS RESULTING
FROM SYNCHRONIZATION OF RHYTHMS

The notion of synchronization has been with the behavioral and social sciences for a relatively long time. Many theories in those fields are based on the idea of a static equilibrium, fluctuating around a fixed set point, or steady state; and problems of coordination or synchronization of different processes are most often posed in that frame of reference. But the idea of entrainment of rhythms, within the biological sciences, makes it clear that *static* equilibrium models will not suffice for the dynamic phenomena of those biological—and our behavioral—fields. What is needed is a model involving "dynamic equilibrium" in which the specific process pattern(s), that constitute the balanced or steady state for the organism, change over time and do so in systematic ways. For example, a certain balance between food intake and exercise is needed to maintain a certain body weight. But not only may the desired weight (i.e., the set point) change over the course of a lifetime; the very nature of the intake–exercise balance changes over time. As we age, we need to shift to a lower ratio of intake to exercise if we want to maintain any given body weight. Furthermore, that outcome and the balance leading to it may be modified by various external factors: disease, nutrition levels of the food available and used, environmental hazards, and so forth. The particular usefulness of the Social Entrainment Model to the behavioral and social sciences is the notion of dynamic equilibrium that underlies it; that is, the notion that much of human behavior involves patterns of behavior systems that fluctuate, systematically, over time.

The entrainment model can be applied to behavior systems at various levels. The multiple endogenous temporal processes are processes that are inherent in the particular behavior system being examined. These processes tend to become mutually entrained or synchronized, leading to a particular temporal pattern of behavior of that system. Events external to that system can act on either the endogenous processes themselves, or on the synchronization processes by which they become mutually entrained, to alter the temporal patterns of behavior for that behavior system. Such an entrainment model can apply not only to systems made up of physiological processes, but also to systems of psychological processes at the individual level, and to systems of social-psychological processes for interacting dyads, groups, or larger organized social units.

Using the Social Entrainment Model to Examine Social Behavior: Studies of RHYTHM, MESH, and TEMPO

The Social Entrainment Model seems useful in examining, and perhaps extending, the current conceptions in several areas of social psychology. Take, for example, the equilibrium theory of intimacy proposed by Argyle and Dean (1965), Argyle and Kendon (1967), and Kendon (1967). They propose that three behaviors—eye contact (or, more accurately, mutual gaze), body orientation, and distance between interacting partners— constitute a mutually interdependent system that adjusts in a compensatory fashion to establish and maintain a particular level of intimacy for a given situation. We can use the Social Entrainment Model to analyze this formulation from a new perspective. A social entrainment view implies that there are multiple independent patterns of activity by the interacting partners (RHYTHM) that become synchronized in a compensatory fashion (MESH) to establish a pattern of activity that constitutes an appropriate level of intimacy between the two (TEMPO). If an external event (PACE) changed one of those behaviors (e.g., if interactional distance was increased), one or both of the others would adjust in order to reestablish the prior equilibrium.

Altman and colleagues (Altman, 1975; Altman & Taylor, 1973; Altman, Vinsel, & Brown, 1981) have extended their prior work on intimacy and privacy in the form of a single integrated perspective that deals with both intimacy and privacy in terms of a dialectical system of interpersonal boundary regulation. They argue that an equilibrium theory is not an adequate expression of human behavior. There are systematic fluctuations in the desired levels (i.e., in the set points) for privacy and intimacy; and these can be captured better in a model that involves a dynamic patterning. Altman *et al.* argue that several dialectical processes that change over time underlie many fundamental aspects of our social behavior: openness and closedness, intimacy and privacy, and stability and change. That is, people oscillate between desiring more intimacy and desiring more privacy (less intimacy). Similarly, they vary in their desired levels of stability/continuity on the one hand, and change/novelty on the other. Therefore, a description of people's use of boundary-regulation mechanisms for one point in time is not an adequate description of human social behavior. Instead, we must look at fluctuations in the patterning of use of these mechanisms over time. In other words, we need to focus on dynamic patterning—with part of that dynamic patterning entailing systematic change (i.e., oscillations) over time.

The argument posed by Altman and colleagues is consistent with our Social Entrainment Model. Researchers have tried to address the question of how one partner's behavior influences the other partner's behavior. Two principles have been used. One, "reciprocity," implies that increases in certain behaviors (e.g., parts of the intimacy "package" already mentioned, such as smiling or eye contact) are desired *without limit*. Reciprocity implies that increases in any one of these behaviors would be reacted to by further increases. The other principle, "compensation," suggests that there is a certain desired steady state or equilibrium pattern for the behavior variables related to the regulation of interaction. What our model would argue, and what Altman and colleagues would argue, is that any such equilibrium point or pattern would itself fluctuate over time, perhaps in a cyclical fashion. Therefore, the effects of one partner's behavior on the other partner's behavior will depend in part on its timing, that is, on the phase and periodicity of the partner's actual and desired activity levels, and perhaps on other endogenous rhythms as well.

ENTRAINMENT IN CONVERSATION

Research on temporal patterns of speech has obtained findings consistent with the Social Entrainment Model. Although there is some controversy about whether or not sequencing of utterances and pauses is rhythmically structured (Warner, 1979), most researchers agree that some sort of adjustment or accommodation takes place between conversational partners during an interaction. Chapple (1970) identifies this accommodation as "mutual entrainment." According to Chapple, mutual entrainment occurs when the interactional partners' periods of interaction are equal and when their phase is shifted one-half turn apart (that is, opposite phase). Within a typical conversation, the peak of person A's activity occurs in temporal conjunction with the lowest level of person B's activity level, and vice versa. When interaction of a dyad is considered over a period of days, however (Hayes & Cobb, 1979), the partners' activity levels are exactly in phase with each other. The two members of a dyad are both active (talking) during certain periods, and are both not talking during other periods. The idea of coordination of behavior by the two interacting partners holds throughout these different phases of their interaction, but the specific meaning of coordination, or synchronization, differs.

Chapple (1970) also points out that mutual entrainment might not always be possible. When the baseline for preferred activity levels between two people are strikingly different, mutual entrainment is not likely to occur. The adjustment necessary for the two partners is just too large. This is related to what Moore-Ede and colleagues call the range of entrainment in regard to physiological rhythms (Moore-Ede *et al.*, 1982). There are limits as to how far two or more oscillators can vary from one another in periodicity and still mutually entrain. When the differences are within the partners' range of entrainment, the two partners may not adjust equally; rather, one may simply adapt to the other's activity pattern. Such differences could be used to reckon the relative dominance of the partners. This provides a different definition of interactional dominance than simply amount of talking, the most usual operationalization for dominance. It also is a definition different from the one used by Gottman (1979) in studying conflict in marital couples.

Chapple (1970) suggests that the fit between partners' interactional styles and activity levels may be a basis for interpersonal attraction. That is, people may tend to be more attracted to those people with whom mutual entrainment of interaction patterns is easiest: that is, the smaller the adjustment needed, the more attraction there will be. Warner (1984) cautions, however, that the opposite direction of that relation—that we can achieve mutual entrainment easiest with those for whom we have high attraction—is equally plausible.

ENTRAINMENT IN GROUP SETTINGS

Some aspects of the classic work of Bales (1950) on group interaction process also can be tied to our social entrainment model. Bales used his interaction process analysis (IPA) system to explore the task and interpersonal aspects of communication within small, problem-solving groups. He assumed the operation of forces toward equilibrium between the instrumental (i.e., task) and the expressive (i.e., socioemotional) activities of the group. In this view, task-oriented activities give rise to tensions in the socioemotional area. When the group turns its attention to those issues, neglect of task performance in turn gives rise to task-related tensions. Thus, the group oscillates between these two major foci of activity, *in the service of an equilibrium that will minimize or eliminate tension in the system*. It is hard to assess the plausibility of such an equilibrium interpretation of the interaction process. Such an equilibrium process was assumed, rather than tested, in the empirical work using Bales's IPA. The same evidence can be used to support another interpretation with more or less equal plausibility. We can view the interaction sequence in such groups as a straightforward task-activity sequence that is punctuated, periodically, by positive and negative socioemotional activities.

Another temporal feature within Bales's interaction system, the "phase-movement hypothesis," is more testable, and perhaps more interesting. Bales hypothesized that a typical problem-solving group is characterized by three shifts in task activities: (1) a high amount of activity involving task orientation at the outset, with a decline in the relative amount of such activity thereafter; (2) a (relatively) high amount of activity involving task evaluation during the middle part of the group's work, with lower levels of evaluation in preceding and following phases; and (3) a (relatively) high amount of activity involving task control during the final portion of the group's work, following a steady rise from low levels of such activity at the outset. Along with these patterned sequences of task activity, Bales posited an increase, from beginning to end of the session, in both positive and negative socioemotional activities (with a slight downturn in negative ones and an upturn in positive ones in the very last part of the session). The hypothesis that there is a systematic pattern of task activities over phases of the session tends to be supported by the empirical results for studies in which the group meets for only one session and attempts to complete its tasks within that session (which was the case for almost all of the studies done by Bales and his group). Such a phase movement does not hold, apparently, for groups that take on tasks extending over more than one meeting. Whether or not there is the hypothesized increase in socioemotional activity over this same phase sequence is less clear-cut because—in virtually all studies of such matters—the base rates for all categories except the main active task activities are extremely low.

Work on overstaffing and understaffing of behavior settings (e.g., Wicker, 1979) can also be construed as entrainment-related phenomena. A behavior setting includes multiple ac-

tors, multiple tasks, and a desired pattern of coordination between the two (so that the requirements of the setting are in
fact met, that is, so that the setting "comes off"). Under- or
overstaffing disturbs the desired pattern of coordination, hence
reducing the efficiency of operation of the behavior setting.
When the setting is understaffed, key tasks of the setting may
go undone; and individuals are liable to undertake more tasks
and work harder at them (i.e., increase their productivity *rate*
per person). When the setting is overstaffed, there is much
"empty" time (in regard to performance of task requirements
of the setting), and setting inhabitants are more selective in
what tasks they tackle, and more evaluative in their views of
their own and others' performance (hence, setting higher
standards of performance quality).

CONCLUDING COMMENTS

The point of this discussion is to show that the entrainment
model is applicable to research in a number of problem areas
at the group as well as the individual level. Thus far, most of
the discussion has dealt with the first three components of the
model—RHYTHM, MESH, and TEMPO. In the next section
of this chapter, we will turn to an examination of the fourth
(PACE) component of the model, the part within which most
of the empirical research of our own program has been concentrated. In particular, we will examine how time limits affect
the patterns of task performance of groups and individuals
and the patterns of interaction within those groups.

EXTERNAL ENTRAINMENT IN GROUP INTERACTION
AND TASK PERFORMANCE:
STUDIES OF PACE

Individuals and groups perform tasks of various kinds in industrial, educational, governmental, recreational, familial, and
other settings. Sometimes these tasks are done at leisure,
sometimes they are paced by an outside time, and sometimes

they are done as fast as possible. Parkinson's famous first law (Parkinson, 1957) asserts that "work expands to fill the time available for it." We prefer to view his evidence and the many other cases to which his law would seem to apply as cases of temporal entrainment: work is done at a pace that fits the dominant rhythms present in the situation. Or, to put the matter in other words, we do what we have to do in the time we have to do it.

Such entrainment is by no means all on the sloth side, as Parkinson's general tone, if not his exact statements, would have us infer. If work expands to fill the time available for it, then might it not also contract to fit a scarcer time? We might worry about such contraction on the grounds that surely work done much faster than usual would be slipshod and full of errors. But we seem not to expect, in the converse case, that work expanded to fit plentiful time will be improved in quality.

Actually, there has been little research on any of these several hypothesized relations. We have recently conducted several studies to examine these relations, and we are currently conducting several more. In one completed study, we found remarkably regular functions for rates of performance over time. The results of that study shed some light on questions of temporal entrainment of task performance and are summarized very briefly in the paragraphs to follow (see Kelly, 1984; Kelly & McGrath, 1983; Kelly & McGrath, 1985; McGrath, Kelly, & Machatka, 1984, for more details on these studies).

A series of two-person groups worked in one or another of each of three task-load conditions and in one or another of each of three time-interval conditions, using a task requiring the solution of a series of five-letter anagrams. We also had four-person groups and "one-person groups" work in some but not all of those nine conditions. Each group had either 20, 40, or 80 anagrams to solve, and, for the first work period, had either 5, 10, or 20 minutes to solve as many of them as they could. Each group had three work periods, with the task load remaining the same for all three periods but with the time interval varying as follows. Groups that began with a 5-minute interval had 10, then 20 minutes on the other two work periods. Groups that began with a 20-minute interval then had

10 and 5 minutes on the other two trials. Groups that began with 10 minutes had two more 10-minute trials. For those cells in which we had individuals and four-person groups, as well as dyads, we could compare the effect of changes in task load, in time interval, and in group size, and look at the results in terms of trade-offs assessed in standard performance units comparable across conditions ("anagrams solved per member per minute").

Although we had relatively small samples in each cell, the results for anagram task performance were strikingly regular. First, groups of any given size solved more anagrams per member-minute the higher the assigned task load. The more work they were given in a given time period, the more they did; or, to put the matter in Parkinson's terms, the less work they were given the less they did in any given time period. Second, the shorter the time limit on the work period, the higher the *rate* (that is, anagrams solved per member per minute) at which they solved the anagrams. Here, clearly, work *contracts* to fit the time available, or it expands to fill the time available, whichever you prefer. Third, the smaller the group, the higher the rate at which anagrams got solved. Individuals were much faster, on a member-minute basis, than dyads; and dyads in turn were much faster than tetrads. This is, of course, in accord with a long history of research on group size and group productivity and fits nicely with Steiner's notions of coordination losses (Steiner, 1972). Those functions, too, are quite regular; and their fit to past research and their regularity give us confidence in the other results in spite of the small samples on which they are based.

But we had one other set of findings, unanticipated and quite interesting. People in the conditions that began with the shortest time limit and had longer time limits in successive work periods performed at faster rates, in every condition (that is for every group size, every task load), than those in conditions that began with a long time limit and had shorter and shorter work times for successive trials. The people who had three successive work periods with the same time limit had rates between the other two conditions for the comparable loads and intervals. Specifically, the dyads who had a given task load and the 5-, 10-, 20-minute sequence solved more anagrams in *each* of those work periods than did the groups with the 20-, 10-, 5-minute sequence in the comparable intervals. In fact, the people who started with a 5-minute time limit solved more anagrams in *any given minute* (e.g., in the 1st, or the 6th, or the 14th minute of a trial of a certain length/load) than did the people who started with a 20-minute time limit. Again, the people who started with (and continued with) a 10-minute period scored between the other two groups in each comparable minute. It was as if the initial time limit assigned to the group somehow established a "frame of reference" (to use a term from the earlier years of our field), or a "set of expectations" (to use a more modern term), or a "set point" (to borrow from biological psychology), or, to use our own preferred term, a "temporal entrainment" of the task performance process.

Keep in mind that this pattern of entrainment held for groups of different sizes and for each of the three task loads; that it held in the face of presumed learning effects (at least learning to coordinate with one another, if not learning to do anagrams better) and fatigue effects (which seemed to set in for third work period); and that it held for each parallel minute of the work time. It also held for two recent replications that included different time intervals and different sizes of anagram (four, five, and six letters). The groups that had three 10-minute trials showed what looked like slight learning effects from first to second work period, and slight fatigue effects from second to third. But the *second trial* performance of the groups that started with the 5-minute limit were better than those of the groups that started with a 20-minute first trial (and the 10-minute first trial groups were again in between). Those second trials were all of 10-minute length for all conditions. The conditions differed in their second trial rates and (as far as we know) they otherwise differed only in their first trial time limits. Their second trial performance rates varied in accord with whether they had been given a longer, a shorter, or the same length time limit for that second trial than they had "gotten used to" in trial one.

There are other potential interpretations that would fit the results. We prefer an interpretation based on the idea of *entrainment*. That is, we want to regard these findings as an indication that *groups and individuals attune their rates of work to fit the temporal conditions of their work situations, and that such attunement, once established, persists to some degree even when surrounding temporal conditions have changed.* We believe that if we ran groups in a longer series of similar trials, they would eventually adapt from their initial *set point* to one more appropriate to trial conditions (that is, they would slow down their rate if there was more than enough time, speed it up if there was less than enough time, and so forth). While the latter statement would be in support of Parkinson's principle, and of its opposite (that is, that work contracts to fit the available time), we find its implications far more exciting and of far more potential importance when we regard it as evidence of temporal entrainment of individual and group task performances.

The temporal entrainment of task performance, and in particular of work rates, points to another interesting question: What kind of entrainment effects are there on patterns of interaction? If we take as truth, for the moment, the hypothesis that work actually does contract and expand to fit the time available for it, then we might ask what it is that does not get done when time is scarce, and what gets overdone when time is abundant. For example, when time is short, do groups cut out all task-irrelevant interaction in order to complete the work; and, if so, what are the consequences of such a strong task focus for the subsequent performance of, and interaction within, those groups? Conversely, when time is plentiful, do groups engage in more interpersonal interaction; and, if so, what are the consequences of such an interpersonal focus for future performance and interaction in those groups?

Kelly (1984; Kelly & McGrath, 1985) explored these questions in a study in which groups of four (and individuals) were given two tasks to complete, one in each of two time periods. Three different task types (adapted from Hackman, 1968) were used, although any given group worked on two tasks of the same type. All three task types required the group to produce a written solution to a problem. Production tasks required the group to generate ideas relating to an assigned topic. Discussion tasks required the group to discuss a certain assigned issue and reach a resolution of it. Planning tasks required the group to come up with a plan of action to accomplish a certain assigned goal. Two orders of time periods were used. Half of the groups worked on the first task for 10 minutes and the second task for 20 minutes. The other half of the groups worked first for 20 minutes, then for 10. An observer recorded what kind of behavior was occurring *at the 10-th second of each 10-second interval* throughout the two task-performance periods. Each observation was coded into one of eight categories: answers, questions, agreements, disagreements, positive interpersonal comments, negative interpersonal comments, neutral comments, and silence.

To explore the question of temporal entrainment, the interaction data were analyzed by log-linear tests of the distributions of frequencies over the eight categories, as a function of task type, time limit, and time order. (For a more detailed description of methods and results, see Kelly, 1984).

On the first task, the interaction pattern differed as a function of length of time interval. There were relatively more disagreements, positive interpersonal comments, and negative interpersonal comments for groups with the longer (20-minute) time interval on their first tasks. This pattern was *reversed*, however, for the second task, for which there were proportionally more disagreements, positive interpersonal comments, and negative interpersonal comments for the groups with the 10-minute time interval. Note that the 10-minute second sessions all had been preceded by a 20-minute first session, while the 20-minute second sessions all had been preceded by a 10-minute first session. Furthermore, the chi-square for comparisons of the two consecutive sessions of the same groups are relatively small for the groups in the 10-minute–20-minute condition, and are nonsignificant for the groups in the 20-minute–10-minute condition. These results suggest: (1) that the pattern of interaction in the first session is determined, at least in part, by the time limit imposed on the group's work; and (2) that certain features of the pattern of interaction that are set in a group's first task session carry over into a second task session. In other words, features of interaction are entrained to an externally imposed temporal constraint, and that entrainment persists beyond the single task performance. (See Kelly, 1984, and Kelly & McGrath, 1985, for more detail on these findings, for the interaction analysis by task type, and for the analysis of task performances.)

This study demonstrates that the interaction patterns of groups may be subject to entrainment effects from externally imposed task and time requirements. Tentatively, shorter time limits may be conducive to more concentration on task-oriented behavior. The group seems to spend more time working on the task itself, and less time engaged in task-irrelevant interactions. With longer time intervals to work on a task, groups engage in more interpersonal interaction.

While this may seem like a prescription for gaining task efficiency and saving worker-hours as well, by placing stringent temporal requirements on the group, it may well offer a short-term profit at a high long-term cost. There is considerable evidence from research on restricted communication channels in work groups, for example, that groups need "broad-band" communications, including interpersonal communications, for effective task performance on many types of tasks (see Mc-Grath, 1984 for a summary of that work). Furthermore, for groups with some continuity over time (a past and/or a future), a certain amount of interpersonal interaction is necessary to build group performance norms that, in turn, can greatly increase the efficiency of later group task performance.

A further cost involves the effects of higher performance *rates* on the *quality* of task performance. Kelly and McGrath (1985) found that shorter time limits elicited increased rates of performance, in terms of number of words per minute. (Note that this increased rate also can be predicted from the much-studied goal-setting model.) But they also found that such shorter time limits were accompanied by lower quality of performance, in terms of creativity, originality, and the quality of presentation. This was true for all three task types used, and for both individuals and groups. (Goal-setting theory is silent as to performance quality.) Thus, there is a trade-off between some aspects of quality (e.g., creativity) and some aspects of quantity (e.g., solution rate per person per minute). For tasks in which sheer amount of work is the only desideratum, decreased time limits may result in better performance. But for tasks in which quality counts as well, time pressure may prove to be both boon and bane.

Concluding Comments

The Social Entrainment Model provides an exciting conceptual framework for integrating previous research and suggesting avenues for future work. In particular, it provides a way to conceptualize more dynamic patterns of human behavior. The research in our field has been all too static. Even attempts at examining the more dynamic aspects of behavior, such as interpersonal interaction process, have tended to resort to summary statements that collapse information over the temporal dimension. However, many interesting aspects of behavior can be seen only by looking at patterns of behavior over relatively micro level units of time.

What is clear from these results is that both task-performance patterns and social-interaction patterns—like many physiological and psychological patterns at the individual level—are very sensitive to both internal and external time pacers and rhythms. People in interaction entrain one another; and their mutually entrained patterns of task performance and interaction in turn become entrained to external temporal markers and cycles. These internal and external rhythms abound in work organizations, both at the relatively micro levels to which we have been attending thus far, and at the more macro levels of work schedules and role performances to which we will turn in the next chapter.

C H A P T E R 5

Time and Work

People spend a lot of their time in organizations. Some of those organizations are designed for work and some are designed for other activities. This chapter is about how temporal factors play a part in the relation of the individual to those organizations. We examine the individual's and the organization's views of temporal issues—perspectives sometimes in conflict. We then consider the entrainment of time away from work to time at work and the effects of this phenomenon on the lives of workers and the people in their social networks.

TIME-BASED STRESS IN WORK ORGANIZATIONS

At least three fundamental problems are inherent in collective action: uncertainty, conflicting interests, and inherent scarcity of resources. Each of these problems has a temporal aspect. Each of them gives rise to certain temporal issues for the collective (and here, we will focus on collectives that are formal work organizations). Organizations deal with such temporal issues in characteristic ways suited to their needs and circumstances. Each of these inherent temporal problems also gives rise to certain somewhat different temporal issues for the individuals who are members of that collective, that organiza-

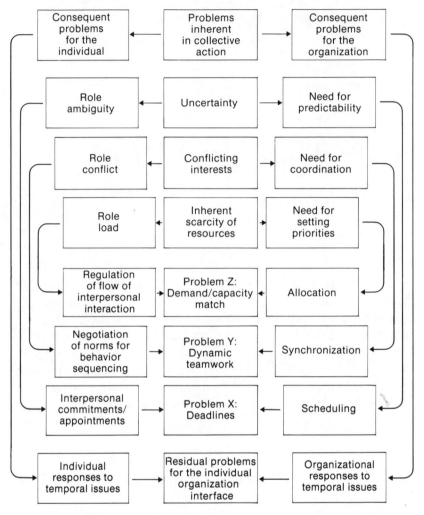

Consequent problems for the individual	Problems inherent in collective action	Consequent problems for the organization
Role ambiguity	Uncertainty	Need for predictability
Role conflict	Conflicting interests	Need for coordination
Role load	Inherent scarcity of resources	Need for setting priorities
Regulation of flow of interpersonal interaction	Problem Z: Demand/capacity match	Allocation
Negotiation of norms for behavior sequencing	Problem Y: Dynamic teamwork	Synchronization
Interpersonal commitments/ appointments	Problem X: Deadlines	Scheduling
Individual responses to temporal issues	Residual problems for the individual organization interface	Organizational responses to temporal issues

Figure 5-1. Temporal issues in organizations.

tion. Individuals also deal with such temporal issues in characteristic ways suited to their own needs and circumstances.

These two sets of responses—by the organization and by its individual members—are seldom, if ever, totally compatible. The juxtaposition of the organization's solutions to the temporal problems, and the individual's solutions to them, identifies a new set of problems—at the point where the organization and the individual interface. These problems of fit represent continuing problems for both individuals and organizations. To some degree, they reflect the different goals, priorities, and criteria of individuals and the organizations in which they work. But to some degree, they also reflect the clash of conflicting conceptions of time—different time frames that we have called, in an earlier chapter, "organizational time" and "Transactional time." These relations are illustrated in Figure 5-1, and are discussed in this section.

TEMPORAL ISSUES FOR THE ORGANIZATION

A number of scholars have argued that the time orientation of modern industrialized culture was shaped by factors that accompanied the industrial revolution (e.g., deGrazia, 1972; Dubin, 1973; Lakoff & Johnson, 1980; Moore, 1963). In any case, large work organizations of the kinds that began to emerge during that period are often characterized by high levels of functional specialization, segmentation of positions and roles, and separation of parts in both time and space. Such specialization, segmentation, and separation creates the need for extensive coordination, in space and time, among the many activities of various parts of the organization, and between those organizational activities and the actions of various units outside of—but having important relations with—the organization (e.g., suppliers, customers, and so forth). Coordination requires plans; temporal coordination requires predictable schedules; prediction requires measurements; and precise prediction and coordination requires precise measurements.

Thus, specialization breeds segmentation and separation; those require coordination, which in turn implies plans, including time schedules; schedules require accurate temporal prediction, and accurate prediction requires accurate measurement of time.

The clock thus becomes a major instrument for coordination and control, and human parts of the organization must adapt to (i.e., become entrained to) work schedules. This increased emphasis on time also implies a time-based definition of units of work and a time-based conceptualization of the work–worker relation. Before the industrial revolution, our culture had what Graham (1981) calls a *"procedural–traditional"* temporal orientation, within which the natural unit of work was the completed task. Since then, the dominant time orientation has been one that Graham calls a *"linear–separable"* orientation and that we call organizational time. In that orientation, the natural unit of work is the "manhour" [*sic*]. That orientation also stresses a particular view of the employer–employee relation: Time, rather than effort or skill, is what the worker contributes in the work relation; and time, rather than skill or effort, is what is paid for in the work exchange. If what is contributed, and paid for, is the worker's time, then time—like money—becomes a valuable, tangible commodity that can be saved, spent, earned, and counted (deGrazia, 1972).

Lakoff and Johnson (1980) sum up these ideas in a series of three metaphors that they believe characterize the dominant conception of time in modern industrialized cultures: Time is money, time is a limited resource, and time is a valuable commodity. As they note, this view of time is by no means universal across cultures, nor historically continuous even within the cultures for which it is now the dominant view.

We would amend their first metaphor slightly, as we suggested in an earlier chapter in the discussion of "temponomics." To a large extent, time and money are not as interchangeable as the phrase "time is money" would imply. Rather, they are exchangeable. Time is not money, but it can be turned into money. Money can buy time. Money increases in value over time. Time can be invested now to yield money later. Time, like money, can be counted, spent, saved, wasted, possessed, invested, budgeted, used up, borrowed, lost, left over, and valued (deGrazia, 1972; Graham, 1981; Lakoff & Johnson, 1980; McGrath & Rotchford, 1983; Moore, 1963).

As already suggested, modern-day work organizations are beset by three problems inherent in any attempts to carry out collective action. The first of these is the problem of *inherent uncertainty*, in the relation of the organization to its environment and in the relation of the organization to each of its parts, including the individuals who are its members. This uncertainty implies a need for predictability, including temporal predictability. The need for predictability, in turn, gives rise to the formulation and imposition of plans, including schedules that are the temporal parts of plans.

Typically, such schedules are established centrally and imposed by the organization on its units and members. Furthermore, such schedules tend to be preset; hence, they may prove inflexible in the face of unexpected events or conditions. We will talk about these same two issues later from the individual's point of view: autonomy versus centralization of control; and the static quality of preset plans versus the dynamic quality of ongoing interaction.

The second problem, fundamental to any collective action, is the problem of *conflicting interests*. Whenever there is more than one party, those parties may have different purposes, different goals, different preferences for actions and outcomes. Whenever there are specialized, segmented, and separated parts, those parts may involve activities that require coordination. The existence of or potential for conflicting interests within an organization leads to a need for coordination of activities of the organization's separate parts. This need, in turn, gives rise to efforts toward synchronization (temporal coordination) of activities of all parts of the organization.

Scheduling and synchronization are distinct though related concepts. The essence of scheduling is to determine when some event will occur or some product will be available in relation to an external calendar or clock. In other words, it involves starting times and deadlines that relate organizational activities and events to "real" or "outside" time. As discussed in Chapter 3, this often involves a juxtaposition of two time frames, the organization's "internal" time frame and the general time frame of the surrounding culture. The essence of synchronization is to insure that action "a," by person "i," occurs in a certain relation to the time when action "b" is done by person "j." In other words, synchronization involves the timing of starts and stops of multiple activities, and is a matter of relating organizational activities and events to one another in "organization" or "inside" time. That is, synchronization is an entraining of work rhythms, such that the activities of different people performing their different tasks become coordinated in phase and periodicity.

As with schedules, plans for synchronization tend to be imposed by the organization on its members or unit parts, and such plans tend to involve preset algorithms for effective coordination. Thus, organizational efforts toward synchronization raise the same two issues for the individual–organization interface as did scheduling: autonomy versus centralized control; and the static quality of plans versus the dynamic quality of ongoing interaction.

The third problem fundamental to any collective action is the *inherent scarcity of resources*. In the dominant conception, time is one such scarce resource. This scarcity of time gives rise to a need for the establishment of temporal priorities. Formulation of temporal priorities amounts to an allocation of temporal resources to organizational activities and units. Whereas schedules have to do with when something is to occur in relation to outside time, and synchronization has to do with when something is to occur with respect to some other system activities or events, allocation has to do with how much time is to be devoted to various system activities. The essence of allocation is to assign temporal resources to tasks, hence to give those tasks organizational value, and to assign task responsibilities to staff. As with the other two organizational responses, temporal allocation tends to be imposed by the organization on its members and unit parts, and to be preset and therefore not very responsive to ongoing events. And, as with the other two organizational responses, allocations also tend to pose the same two issues, of autonomy versus central control, and of static versus dynamic response.

Thus, the three problems inherent in collective action, namely uncertainty, conflicting interests, and scarcity, give rise to three parallel needs on the part of the organization, namely the need for predictability, the need for temporal coordination, and the need for setting priorities. These three needs, in turn, give rise to three prototypical organizational responses: the development of plans and schedules; the development of efforts for synchronization of activities; and the development of a set of allocations of temporal resources to units and activities.

All three of these responses tend to involve preset plans and to be imposed by the organization on its members and units. All three of these responses, therefore, raise two problems for the interface between individual and organization, namely: (1) the problem of individual (or unit) autonomy versus centralized control, and (2) the problem of preset but static plans versus improvised but dynamic reaction to ongoing events.

Those same three inherent problems give rise to a similar chain of needs and responses at the level of the individual member of such organizations. We now turn to a description of those member-level issues.

TEMPORAL ISSUES FOR THE INDIVIDUAL

Any individual who is a member of a large formal organization is usually also a member of the broad culture within which that organization is embedded and from which, at least in part, it draws its temporal conceptions. So those individuals are likely to share that organization's conception of time to some degree. On the other hand, every culture contains subcultures whose value orientations (including their temporal conceptions) are a patterned variant of the culture's dominant value orientation. Subsets of members (and/or of clients) of an organization may come from such a variant subculture and therefore bring with them an alternative value orientation and temporal conception. Graham (1981) argues that a given individual is likely to have "command of" more than one of these time conceptions, and to choose one or another of them as an operating culture for a given set of activities.

We arrive at a similar position by a different route. For the most part, members of organizations certainly understand, have command of, the temporal perspective we call organizational time. That is the dominant conception of time that drives organizational affairs. At the same time, individuals understand and have command of other time conceptions as well—ones that the culture endorses for use under certain circumstances. They probably have command, for example, of a Newtonian time that they could use for certain mathematical or logical purposes. They probably also have command of at least some of the ideas of Einsteinian time (e.g., the idea of relativity, or the idea of entropy). And they certainly appreciate time's epochality in relation to a number of personal time markers such as birthdays, anniversaries, and special occasions. We would argue that they also have a command of the Transactional time conception that is used for interpersonal interaction. Furthermore, interactional or Transactional time is the appropriate time conception to use in structuring interpersonal interactions or other social behavior—whereas organizational time is the appropriate conception to use in structuring task or instrumental activities. The organization intends to deal with (and to deal only with) task-instrumental activities, and to do so in organizational time. But the individual within the organization must deal to a very large extent with interpersonal activities (even when executing his or her tasks), and tends to deal with those interpersonal activities in terms of interactional time. The juxtaposition of two different temporal frames of reference makes for some problems of fit for the individual in relation to the organization.

The three problems inherent in collective action pose distinctive problems for individuals who are members of such organizations. These problems are quite parallel to the set of problems that has been studied as the three main sources of role-based stress in organizational settings (Kahn et al., 1964). From the individual point of view, the problem of uncertainty gives rise to role ambiguity; the problem of conflicting interests underlies the individual problem of role conflict; and the problem of inherent scarcity underlies the problem of role load. Each of these problems has its temporal aspect. The temporal aspect of role ambiguity is knowing precisely when to do specific role behaviors. The temporal aspect of role conflict is knowing which of two or more competing role behaviors to do at a specific time. The temporal aspect of role overload is having more role behaviors to do than can be done in a given time period (or, the other side of the same issue, having too little time allocated for a fixed set of role activities).

At the individual level, then, the three generic problems get translated into the three forms of time-based role stress:

ambiguity, conflict, and load. These, in turn, call forth prototypical responses by individuals that are different from the prototypical responses at the organization level. First, the generic problem of uncertainty, and its individual temporal counterpart, temporal role ambiguity, is dealt with by working out a series of interpersonal commitments. For the temporal aspects of uncertainty and role ambiguity, these interpersonal commitments amount to appointments—jointly negotiated mutual deadlines. Second, the generic problem of conflicting interests and its individual temporal counterpart, temporal role conflict, is dealt with by negotiating a series of interpersonal or behavioral norms that help members coregulate response sequences by which they will carry out their interpersonal interactions. This is akin to the development of interpersonal norms within Thibaut and Kelley's (1959) exchange theory. Third, the generic problem of scarcity and its individual temporal counterpart, temporal role load, is dealt with by developing a variety of stratagems that serve to regulate the flow of interpersonal interaction. Altman (1975) describes such processes in his analysis of privacy and interpersonal boundary regulation.

The latter problem raises some additional considerations. We have phrased the third generic problem in terms of scarcity of resources (and scarcity of time). But we have posed the problem from the individual's point of view as role load, and we have posited the individual's prototypical response to be the regulation of the flow of interaction. Both of the latter concepts—role load and boundary regulation—are *bidirectional*, at least in principle. They both reckon with the possibility of either scarcity or abundance. That is, role-load problems can involve underload as well as overload (Kahn *et al.*, 1964; McGrath, 1970); and boundary-regulation problems can involve a reaching out for more contact (avoiding isolation) as well as a shutting off of too much contact (preserving privacy) (Altman, 1975; Altman *et al.*, 1981).

Those bidirectional concepts invite us to consider rephrasing the generic question bidirectionally as well. Perhaps we should talk about scarcity or overabundance of resources, including temporal resources. This certainly would work at the individual level. Having too much time (in the short run), as well as having too little time, is a frequent part of the human experience of time. A similar bidirectional view of allocation of temporal resources at the organizational level is reflected in the work on overstaffing and understaffing of behavior settings, mentioned in the preceding chapter (Wicker, 1979).

The idea that time can be either scarce or overabundant, at either the organizational or individual level, brings up the dual form of the economic metaphor that we called "temponomics" in Chapter 3. One form of that metaphor—a "scarcity" temponomics—concentrates on saving time or not wasting it. The other form—a "supply side" temponomics—implies an abundance, or at least a steady resupply, of time; and concentrates on spending and investing it rather than saving and avoiding waste. The latter, "supply side" view of time offers one possible way of reducing some of the residual temporal problems at the individual–organization interface by reconceptualizing how organizational tasks get "chunked," assigned, and monitored (which will be discussed in the last part of this section).

In any case, at the interpersonal level, the prototypical response to the "amount of time available"—that is, both its inherent scarcity and its inexorable flow and continuous availability—is the development of techniques for regulating the flow of interpersonal interaction, taking into account both its scarcity and value on the one hand, and its abundance and inexorable availability on the other.

RESIDUAL PROBLEMS AT THE INDIVIDUAL–ORGANIZATION
INTERFACE

As suggested earlier in the chapter, and as indicated in Figure 5-1, the solutions generated at the organizational level and those generated at the individual level are not necessarily compatible. Indeed, it is often the case that what is a solution for a certain temporal problem at one of those levels is the very occasion for such a problem at the other level. For example, an organization might solve a temporal priority problem by asserting that a certain activity, "a," must be done today even if it means the staff working overtime. For the individual, such a "schedule" may create a temporal problem rather than solving one, if the individual has other activities scheduled for that evening. Conversely, an individual might solve a particular personal problem of role overload or conflict (between a work role and a family role, for example) by taking a day's leave from work. The organization may be caught short in a particular skill or service by this unplanned absence. The same action that solved a temporal problem for the individual created one for the organization.

In any case, for all three of the temporal issues, organizational responses tend to be in conflict with the respective individual level responses on at least two important issues. First, all of the organizational level responses tend to be imposed by the organization on its individual members and units. Such centralized control is likely to conflict with the individual's concern for autonomy and/or for voice in decisions affecting his or her work. Second, all of the organizational level responses—virtually by definition—tend to involve preset plans that have a static character when applied in an actual ongoing situation. The individual level responses, on the other hand, all involve patterns of behavior that can be continuously monitored and modified in dynamic reaction to events within the ongoing situation. If the organization fixes its schedule, its synchronization rules, and/or its allocation of temporal resources, and does not allow them to be changed in response to ongoing situations, then those organizational prescriptions will almost certainly clash on some occasions with the interpersonal commitments, behavioral norms, and interaction regulation patterns developed by the individual in response to the same set of temporal problems. If the organization's schedules, synchronization plans, and allocations can be changed on line by individual members in the interest of better dynamic adjustment to ongoing events, then there will almost certainly be a substantial loss in centralized control and an increase in unpredictability of organizational patterns.

We can regard such issues as residual problems at the interface between individual and organization. The residual problems that arise from a lack of fit between the organizational and individual reactions to temporal ambiguity can be grouped as problems having to do with deadlines. The residual problems that arise from lack of fit of organization and individual responses to the problem of conflicting interests can be grouped as problems of "dynamic teamwork"—temporal coordination of activities by continual dynamic mutual synchronization. The residual problems that arise from lack of fit of organization and individual responses to the problem of scarcity (or of scarcity and abundance) can be grouped as problems of demand–capacity match. These three groups of problems—having to do with deadlines, dynamic teamwork, and demand–capacity match—are continuing problems for the organization and its members.

We can get a different view of these residual problems if we take a "supply side" rather than a "scarcity" view of time as an organizational resource. The standard pattern of operation by which work organizations attempt to solve the problem of control is by controlling the work process. In that approach, specific tasks are assigned to specific people, to be done at specific times and places. Task-performance routines are planned with precise synchronization. Schedules are preset and fairly rigidly enforced. Allocation of time and other resources over tasks and roles are made distributively, by itemizing the time requirements of each part of all tasks and roles.

An alternative plan for solving the problem of control is to concentrate on controlling the work results. In this approach, a more global and output-oriented definition of tasks is used. Major projects are assigned to work groups, along with a given set of resources and constraints, with a final deadline specified as one of the constraints (hence, the group's time until that deadline is included as one class of resources). The work group itself is responsible for the subsequent allocation of people, time, and other resources to specific tasks. The work group is accountable to management for having the product by the deadline; but it is not accountable for its itemized work procedures, nor its expenditures of staff time. Such an approach shifts the coin of the employer–employee relation from hours worked to product quantity and quality. At the same time, it can shift both organization and worker to a more balanced or central position on both the centralization versus autonomy issue and on the preset versus dynamic adjustment issue. It would have the organization give up very little control of allocation, regarding who does what projects with what resources by when; some control regarding scheduling; and all control regarding synchronization. Conversely, it would let the individual have full autonomy regarding synchronization, some regarding scheduling, but little regarding allocation. This approach would also keep allocation fairly rigid, permit some flexibility in scheduling, and give full flexibility in regard to synchronization. Such an approach might reduce the residual temporal problems in all three areas.

In part, those three groups of residual problems involve aspects of entrainment. The deadline issues and the whole matter of the organization imposing schedules on its members are related to the idea of entrainment of *phase* of an activity (that is, when the activity will start and/or stop). The dynamic teamwork issues have to do with mutual entrainment of the periodicities of task-performance activity sequences (i.e., the microtemporal structure of the work pattern). The problems involving demand–capacity match are, in a sense, problems of cross-task and/or cross-role conflict or competition. They have to do with the distribution of amounts of effort among a set of tasks and/or roles. They may be closely related to the kinds of entrainment effects we reported in the preceding chapter for individual and group task-performance rates.

These entrainment notions apply to individual and group performance, and to interaction patterns, as indicated in the preceding chapter. Perhaps they apply to the work-role issues discussed here. In the next section of this chapter, we will examine how entrainment effects apply to questions about how work schedules affect the nonwork lives of employees and members of their social networks.

SHIFT WORK: ENTRAINMENT OF NONWORK ROLE BEHAVIORS TO THE WORK SCHEDULE

Consider a worker on regular shift, say the proverbial "nine to five." That schedule ordinarily would be very much in keeping with the person's biological rhythms. He or she would be sleeping when both the temperature and activation cycles are at their lowest, awake and at work when they are high. Furthermore, that individual would be sleeping when everyone else is sleeping and awake and active when others are too. What is more, the stores are open, as are the restaurants, theaters, and other features of life off the job, at times when he or she (and everyone else) can use them fairly conveniently. This is the "natural order" of human life in our culture and in our times (though not necessarily in other cultures nor in other times). From this, one might well infer either that there was no such thing as entrainment, or that all of our lives, like the insects' and plants', are entrained to light, temperature, or other features of the earth's rotational cycle.

But what of the men and women whose jobs put them on the night shift? Their work and wake times are out of synchronization with their (previous) temperature and activity cycles. Their sleep comes when they previously would have been awake. Furthermore—and, we believe, crucially—their sleep comes when other people are awake, while their waking time, on and off the job, comes when other people are either asleep or in other phases of their daily cycles.

The physiological turmoil produced by the de-synchronization of multiple biological rhythms is considerable, and will not have abated entirely by the end of a workweek. At that time, the individual is very likely to go back onto a "normal" schedule of daytime action and nighttime sleep in order to carry out at least some activities in the company of significant others and to do them at times that fit the available time of special resources (such as stores, recreational facilities, and so forth). The next workday brings the physiological turmoil anew, and a new de-synchronization–adaptation cycle begins.

It is probably the case that the physiological rhythms would all, eventually, get resynchronized with one another and with activity and temperature cycles if only the individual did not regress to daytime schedules on weekends. But it is also the case that the social rhythms—of the individual in relation to others in his or her surroundings—would remain out of synchronization for the night worker indefinitely. It is possible to lead a continuing life as a "night person," but if it is to be anything like a full life, one needs to have a whole night community within which to lead it (Melbin, 1978).

The fact of the matter is, of course, that our lives are strongly entrained to temporal rhythms not of our own making and often not noticed. Such entrainment is the case whether we are working night shift or on what we usually regard as normal work shifts. We are less likely to be aware of them, and certainly less likely to be hampered by their constraints, when they are part of the temporal pattern to which all of the surrounding social system is attuned. But our lives are entrained to them, nonetheless.

Consider "rush hour"—that ultimate traumatic by-product of multiple, independent, locally rational decisions about work schedules and arrival times. It seems to most of us most of the time that rush hours are, if not God given, certainly as inevitable as death and taxes. But when we step back from it, we can recognize that the hours that constitute "rush hour," in any particular city and in any particular season, and indeed the very occurrence of a traffic jam related to work arrival and departure times, is a quintessentially human-caused problem that—at least in principle—need not occur at all. There is no reason inherent in the work itself why *all* forms of work must stop and start at closely coordinated times. The reasons why they must be coordinated—thereby producing rush hours— are *social* reasons.

The entraining effects of many features of our culture go virtually unnoticed so long as the observer is on a normal schedule—that is, so long as he or she is thoroughly entrained to the same phase and periodicity as everyone else in the immediate environment. (The plants don't know they are entrained, either, until the researcher messes around with their days and nights!) But, in fact, our normal daily lives are full of rhythms, cycles, periodicities that alter when and how we do what we do. These are so taken-for-granted that it is hard to be convincing about the importance of these phenomena for normal everyday conditions. But the importance is clear enough if we consider shift work and its effects on the worker and his or her family.

We have reviewed a substantial portion of the research

literature on effects of shift work on the lives of workers and their families (see Machatka, 1983; McGrath *et al.*, 1984). We tried to give special emphasis to studies exploring effects of shift work on sleep, health, relations with children and spouse, social and recreational activity, participation in organizations, and satisfaction with job and with life in general. From that review, several things are clear: (1) there are major effects in all of those areas; (2) the effects differ for different temporal patterns imposed by the shift (e.g., night work vs evening work vs rotating work shifts); and (3) the effects probably differ as a function of the worker's age, job tenure, marital and family status, and many other personal characteristics.

We also noted some very serious limitations of past research as reflected in the shift work literature we reviewed. First, past work has concentrated heavily on white male workers, with little attention to female workers or to workers who are members of minority subcultures. Second, very little of this research has been done on the impact of work schedules in relation to the multiple schedules within a family unit (spouse and children). Third, most of that research has concentrated on daily and weekly cycles of work. Very little of it has reflected attempts to trace out the ways in which individuals and families match up units of time with subsets of activities when one or both of them has an off-time work schedule. That is, the research is not at what we might call the microtemporal level. On the other hand, that research also does not reflect work at the macrotemporal level. It does not deal with very long-term cycles (such as developmental and role-change patterns), or even annual or seasonal cycles (such as summer vacation patterns). More work is needed, we believe, at both micro- and macrotemporal levels, and for more heterogeneous populations, on the effects of working off-time shifts.

For those interested in that research literature, a representative sample of some of the best of that work would include the following: Aschoff (1981), Banks (1956), Blakelock (1960), Colquhoun, Blake, and Edwards (1968a, 1968b, 1969), DeLaMare and Walker (1968), Gordan, McGill, and Maltese (1981), Johnson, Tepas, Colquhoun, and Colligan (1981), Maric (1977), Maurice (1975), Melbin (1978), Mott (1978), Mott, Mann,

McLoughlin, and Warwick (1965), Nord and Costigan (1973), Reinberg, Andlauer, and Vieux (1981), Robinson and Converse (1972), Sergean (1971), Tasto, Colligan, Skjei, and Polly (1978), Walker (1978), and Wever (1981).

We can begin to see the pattern involved in work-shift effects by asking how both work and other sets of activities are fit into different phases of a day when an individual is working a normal versus an off-time work shift. For that purpose, we can divide each day into three major phases of roughly equal duration (i.e., 8 hours): day, evening and night. We can also divide activities into three major sets: work (W), rest (R), and everything else (L)—personal, recreational, and social activity. Some have used the term "leisure" and the symbol (L) as an overall rubric for the third category. We will use the same symbol (L), but want it to stand for the term "life activities," which seems a broader and therefore more appropriate label for that category.

There are six possible patterns in which the three parts of the day (daytime, evening, and night) and the three major sets of activities (W, R, L) can be matched. The shift-work literature suggests that there is a sharply defined preference order among those patterns (see Table 5-1).

Given daytime work, virtually all workers use the order W, L, R, for day, evening, and night (pattern 1). When they work day shift, they sleep at night and use the in-between time for other life activities. The alternative order, given that

Table 5-1. Preference Orders for Time–Activity Matching

Preference order for time–activity patterns	Temporal phases of the day		
	Day	Evening	Night
Pattern 1	W	L	R
Pattern 2	L	W	R
Pattern 3	R	L	W
Pattern 4	L	R	W
Pattern 5	R	W	L
Pattern 6	W	R	L

Note: W = Work shift, L = Life activities, R = Rest.

work is in the daytime, puts rest in the evening and life activities at night (W, R, L), and is essentially never used (pattern 6).

When work is fixed on the evening shift, the almost universal pattern (pattern 2) is to rest at night and use day for life activities (L, W, R). The alternative, given that work is to be in evening, puts life activities at night and rest in daytime (R, W, L), and is virtually never used (pattern 5).

When work is fixed at night, the most preferred pattern is to put rest in daytime and life activities in evenings (R, L, W); it is used by about 75% of night-shift workers (pattern 3). The alternative, given night-shift work, is to use day for life activities and evening for rest (L, R, W); this is preferred by about 25% of night workers (pattern 4).

This strong preference order suggests several features of temporal patterns. First, different "chunks" of time are differentially versatile; some, like evenings, can be used for many things; but others, like nighttime, cannot easily be used for certain kinds of activities. Conversely, subsets of activities have different degrees of temporal flexibility; that is, activities vary in the degree to which they can be done at different times.

Those two concepts—"versatility" of portions of time with respect to what activities can be done in them, and "flexibility" of sets of activities with respect to the times when they can be done—allow us to consider the preference orders shown in Table 5-1 in a different way. Its most striking feature is that the *low versatility of night* dominates the preference order. If R is at night, either order of the other two (L and W) gives a highly preferred pattern (1st and 2nd). If R is not at night, then the preference of the other patterns depends on what is put at night. Nighttime not only "prefers" rest as its proper activity; it is also less amenable for life activities than it is for work.

A second striking feature of the preference order is that L is less flexible than W. When either R or W has been assigned to night, it is the location of L (evening preferred) that determines the preference order of the available alternatives.

We can see these features better, perhaps, if we regard these six sequences as being driven by the temporal fixing of

R, or of L, instead of thinking of them only as driven by the work schedule. If we fix R at night (its rightful place!), the two available orders are both quite high: W, L, R, and L, W, R (1st and 2nd orders). If we fix R at evening, the two possible orders (L, R, W, and W, R, L) tend to be low (4th and 6th). If we fix R in daytime, the two available orders (R, L, W, and R, W, L) tend to be moderate in preference (3rd and 5th).

Similarly, we could take the location of L as the driving force. If we put L in its "proper place," evening, the two available orders are both relatively high (1st and 3rd). If we fix L at night, both of the possible orders are low (5th and 6th). If we fix L at daytime, the two available orders are middle to high (2nd and 4th).

When we view the time–activity patterns in this way, rather than assuming that W dominates our lives, it appears that the patterns can be accounted for by the *low versatility of night*, the *low flexibility of R*, and the *low flexibility of L*. This would argue that night work causes problems *not because W was moved from day* (W being flexible and day being versatile), but because *something other than R was put in night time*, which in turn means that *some time other than night was assigned for R*; and/or because *some time other than evening was devoted to L*.

The ideas of versatility of units of time and temporal flexibility of sets of activities are useful, also, when we consider schedules involving longer time units, such as those that change the relation of weekend time to the workweek. Some studies have explored the effects of complex workweeks, such arrangements as a 4-day 40-hour workweek made up of 4 long workdays and a 3-day weekend, or work schedules involving working on weekend days with equivalent time off on weekdays. Results of those studies suggest that, even though weekend time appears to be relatively versatile time, some activities normally done during weekday evenings (e.g., helping kids with homework) are not necessarily transferable to weekends. That is, some L activities have low flexibility with regard to weekend time periods.

All of this suggests that our assigned work schedules tend to entrain other aspects of our lives, whether that work is done in the normal work shift or some other time phase. If our analysis is correct, the impact of a changed work schedule comes not so much from moving work out of its normal daytime slot—work is a very flexible set of activities—but rather from placing something other than rest in the nighttime hours (which some work schedules require) and/or putting what we have called life activities (by which we mean all nonwork, nonrest activities, personal, social, and recreational) in some time other than its normal evening shift. The greatest impact of all comes when the relatively inflexible life activities are assigned to the relatively nonversatile night period. However much time there is, the night is not an adequate period for socializing with friends, interacting with children, or engaging in many facility-dependent or other-people-dependent activities.

This suggests two other temporal features of the time–activity match, in addition to temporal flexibility of activities and versatility of time units. One is the *temporal elasticity of a set of activities*: the degree to which the activities take more or less time as a function of the circumstances under which they are carried out. This is the central idea of Parkinson's notorious first law, and is also involved in the entrainment effects on task performance discussed in the preceding chapter. It seems to us an important idea, one that deserves more study than it has thus far received.

The other temporal feature of this time–activity match is the degree to which a set of activities can be *aggregated* or *disaggregated* with respect to time. To what extent can a certain set of activities, usually done in one "chunk" of time (for example, cleaning up the house), be divided up and done in a number of smaller time units, distributed over a longer calendar time? Conversely, to what extent can a certain set of activities, usually done a small amount at a time in little chunks of time distributed over time (e.g., preparing sandwiches for tomorrow's lunch), be aggregated and done in one larger portion of time (e.g., preparing all of next week's sandwiches on Sunday night)? Some part of the inflexibility of life activities may arise because some of those activities cannot just all be aggregated into a single large block of time. For example, trading longer weekends for shorter weekday evenings is not necessarily a good trade for workers with children, because, as Machatka (1983) noted, you cannot just defer all parenting activities from the workweek evenings to the Friday that is freed by the long-day 4-day workweek.

The significant features of the temporal patterning of people's lives are probably at a much more micro level than we will capture by dealing only at the level of day–evening–night on the one hand, and work–rest–life activities on the other. For example, even a slight change in job starting or finishing time for a single parent may provide an altogether unmanageable schedule, because it undoes temporally inflexible childcare arrangements. We need to look in a much more fine-grained way at the temporal structure of people's lives in order to find out what kinds of time difficulties arise, and how people cope with them.

We probably can learn a lot about what problems arise from shift work by studying at the level of "day," "evening," and "night" on the one hand, and "work," "rest," and "life activities" on the other. But if we want to learn about how people cope with those schedules and those problems, we probably have to disaggregate days into "Monday mornings" and "lunch hours" and "Friday commuting times," and disaggregate activities into "talking with the kids" and "fixing dinner" and "getting to work" and "watching the news on TV." It is at this micro level, especially, that work may contract and expand to fit the time available for it, that work rates are set in part by how much time there is, and that human beings experience the impact of the entrainments of various rhythms of behavior. It is at this level—"watching the news on TV on Tuesday night"—that we can learn most about the social psychology of time.

CHAPTER 6

Time and the Logic of Method

It is remarkable how much of our research methodology involves time, and in how many ways our studies are vulnerable to problems stemming from temporal factors. Some of these problems involve the basic logic behind our research methods. For instance, a specified temporal order is necessary in order to draw valid inferences about cause and effect. Some of these problems are at the strategic level. For instance, time is an issue in the experimental realism of our research settings. Still other temporal problems can be found at the design level. For instance, many features of our research designs are used to control for threats to the internal validity of our conclusions, and many of those threats to internal validity are temporal in nature (e.g., history, maturation, attrition, and so on). Furthermore, temporal issues are ubiquitous at the method or operations level. Many variables involve the measurement of some temporal features of the focal behaviors—rate, frequency, duration, and the like. Both our measures and our manipulations of variables often involve issues of time order and time intervals. And many measures have particular time requirements (lead and lag features) involved in their use.

With temporal matters so pervasive within our methodology, it is surprising that so little attention has been paid to them. In this chapter, we will try to draw attention to some of the main ways in which temporal issues enter into and affect the logic of our methods of research.

Temporal Factors at the Strategic Level

time order and causal interpretation

One central concern of all social science is the ability to draw valid causal inferences. According to the logic of causal interpretation that has dominated our science (and our culture) since Hume, there must be a known time ordering between two events before one of them can be posited as a potential cause of the other. If event B follows event A in time, we know that event A *may* be the cause of B, and we know even more surely that event B *cannot* be the cause of A. Our chain of causal reasoning must move forward in time. For time to run backward, or for effects and causes to run backward in time, is forbidden in the current conceptions of time (although this is not the case for other abstract conceptions of time, such as in the classical Eastern philosophies). In current social science, if causal time were to run backward, our whole edifice of causal interpretation would collapse.

An alternative way to conceptualize cause and effect is an ahistorical or "systems" view. Under this logic, a number of systemic forces operate simultaneously and in a mutually interdependent fashion. If a change should occur in one of those forces, more or less simultaneous changes in one or more others will take place to reestablish some new form of system equilibrium.

This alternative to the Humean time-order basis of cause–effect relations also gives a very central place to temporal factors. The system position does not permit time to run backward any more than does the standard causal position. It simply downplays the effects of simple causal chains, insisting not so much on an atemporal causation as on a multivariate and multidirectional one. The key feature is in the causal interdependence among multiple systemic forces, all of which act mutually and more or less simultaneously on each other rather than acting unidirectionally and in turn. In any case, it has not yet threatened, let alone replaced, the classical Humean position as the dominant causal logic in our field; and even if it did, that would not greatly alter the temporal issues embedded within that logic.

TIME INTERVALS AND CAUSAL EXPLANATION

We can pursue these questions one step further by considering the role of time in causal explanations (given that we have a sufficiently elaborated time order to make a causal interpretation at all). Consider a system involving a set of events at time 1, another set of events at time 2, still another at time 3, and so on. What our Humean methodology tries to do is isolate one (or each of several) events at time 1 as "cause" and measure its effects on one (or several) of the events at time 2 (or time 3, time 4, etc.). If this is to be construed as a cause–effect relation, it is in the interval between time 1 and time 2 that the causal process must be realized. This is a finite time. More often than not, its duration is left unspecified both in our theoretical hypotheses and in our interpretation of concrete findings. But there is another temporal assumption in our Humean logic: There can be no action at a temporal distance, so to speak. However large or small, there *must* be some finite time between cause and effect. That interval must be *filled*, more or less exactly, with the operation of the causal process(es) involved.

There can be serious interpretive consequences if the duration of this finite time is specified incorrectly. If the interval is set too short, the cause may not yet have had time to yield the intended effects when we attempt to observe them. If the interval is set too long, the effects of interest may have come and gone, or they may already have been altered by counter-forces in the system. The problems are even more serious if the cause–effect relation is other than linear or monotonic. If the effect is cyclic, for example, an incorrect specification of the causal interval can lead us to obtain post measures at a time when the effect is at its low ebb (or at its peak), thus misinterpreting the nature of the causal relation under study.

All of these considerations make it clear that we must specify the duration of intervals necessary and sufficient for the unfolding of causal processes, as well as identify the temporal order of postulated causes and effects. This is often difficult to do. For one thing, there is an intuitive bias in behavioral science (and in our culture) favoring the idea that the closer together a cause and effect are in time (and space), the more confident we can be about the soundness of our causal interpretation. There is some truth in this, of course. The closer together the two are in time, the less opportunity there is for other factors to operate. Hence, the less opportunity for such factors either to enhance or obscure the cause–effect relation we are trying to study. What this ignores, of course, is that some causal processes may take a longer time to unfold than others.

This contiguity bias is a part of the Humean causal argument. In his analysis of causality, Hume arrived at the conclusion that the only *rational* basis we could have for inferring causality from empirical events is temporal or spatial contiguity. But that analysis further concludes that, although rational, this basis is also ultimately inadequate to infer any *necessary* connection between the putative cause and its alleged effect. Our willingness to make such causal inferences, stronger ones than we can logically justify, is, according to the Humean analysis, merely cultural custom. We *want* to make strong causal inferences. Some would argue we *need* to make them, to smooth out the business of living. And since we have no better basis, we tend to accept the only rational—though nonlogical—basis we can find: contiguity in time and/or space.

It is easy to find counterexamples of the temporal contiguity principle. For example, the much debated "sleeper effect" in attitude-change research asserts that, when a persuasive message is delivered by a low-credibility source, the message will not have much impact until enough time has passed so that the source of the message is forgotten (but the message itself is remembered). Here, the interval between the presumed cause, the message, and the predicted effect, attitude change, is long indeed—often a matter of months. And much of the problem in establishing the validity of the sleeper effect comes from the interpretive problems associated with determining this long interval and dealing with the effects of other factors that might come into play during it.

So, temporal relations play an important part in the most crucial tasks of our research methodology, namely, establishing valid inferences about causal relations; and then specifying the duration, nature, and operation of the underlying causal processes involved. This set of issues are more problematic in some fields than in others. For example, chemists are very careful in specifying the time period needed for a chemical reaction to take place. Furthermore, they also sometimes have visible markers of the completion of the reaction—a puff of smoke, an explosion, a color change in the solutions. Psychologists seldom have such visible signs of the completion of cognitive, motivational, or affective processes.

TEMPORAL CONSIDERATIONS IN RESEARCH STRATEGIES

Runkel and McGrath (1972) have identified eight classes of research strategies, or settings within which research can be conducted: field studies, field experiments, experimental simulations, laboratory experiments, judgment studies, sample surveys, formal theories, and computer simulations. These strategies can be compared on a number of dimensions, including amount of control, precision of measurement, realism of context, and generalizability over populations. For our purposes here, what is of interest is how each of these strategies treats time.

The strategies differ in terms of how they treat the context within which the behavior being studied is taking place, and they tend to differ in a parallel fashion in terms of how they treat the temporal part of that context. Two of the strategies—

field studies and field experiments—take place in natural settings in which the context is more or less that which naturally occurs in the system under study even when research is not going on. In these, the behavior under study goes forward in what we might call "real time"; that is, the time it takes system events to unfold under normal or natural conditions. Another pair of strategies—experimental simulations and laboratory experiments—take place in what Runkel and McGrath call concocted settings. In these, events unfold within an "experimental time" that is part of the experimental concoction that establishes the context. Two other settings—judgment studies and sample surveys—are done under conditions that attempt to blunt or eliminate the effects of context, thus making the behavior being observed as nearly context free as possible. In these, events do not unfold in time at all. Rather, more or less "timeless" questions get answered in sequences and with time lags that are merely artifacts of the procedures themselves. Finally, the two nonempirical strategies—formal theories and computer simulations—literally have no behavior in them and hence have no temporal behavioral context either. Formal theories may contain important temporal features if such is the content of the theory, but otherwise time enters into them only in a conceptual sense. Computer simulations may contain important temporal process elements within the operation of the model—simulation of system dynamics, for example—but the operation of such temporal processes during a "run" of the simulation does not represent the unfolding of system events, but rather the unfolding of the *model* of system events that is under examination.

Some of the consequences of these differences in treatment of temporal context are worth examination. In field studies, the direct observations that often are the major data-collection tool of that strategy must take place "on line" and in real time. The events being observed are taking place in, and being recorded during, what we can reasonably describe as "natural" temporal patterns. No artificial time constraints are used; the ordering and sequencing of events is left undisturbed. What takes place and when it takes place is determined, not by the concoctions of the experimenter but by the ongoing processes of the real world system that is being studied.

Field experiments, though still taking place in natural settings, add some artificiality to the situation, and some of that artificiality involves temporal features. The settings and behaviors in general are natural with respect to temporal context. However, the experimenter (by design) disturbs the natural ordering of events by manipulation of an independent variable. The behaviors being observed are allowed to unfold in real time, and to follow their natural temporal pattern, *except that* the experimenter has introduced an order relation with respect to one particular set of system events so that a directional causal inference can be made. (Incidentally, such an intervention has the subtle side effect of making the causal-chain interpretation a self-fulfilling prophecy, and making an ahistoric-systemic causal interpretation no longer applicable to the system as it is being studied by this strategy.)

Experimental simulations take the control of temporal orderings one step further. In this strategy, the investigator creates an artificial setting that attempts to mirror the class of natural systems that is being modeled. The experimenter has full control over the introduction of events into the system. In a flight simulator, for example, the experimenter may introduce wind gusts, system failures, an unexpected obstacle, and the like, in any temporal order that suits experimental purposes, to test the operator's and system's reactions to those events. In this strategy the experimenter often makes use of an "experimental time" but tries to *keep it in scale with* real system-operating time, as in the case of the flight simulation in which system response time is crucial. But in other experimental simulations—such as in in-basket tests or mock juries—the experimenter deliberately telescopes the operating time of the simulation so that its experimental time is much more like operating time in laboratory experiments.

Laboratory experiments operate in a totally artificial "experimental time." The time constraints placed on behaviors are often chosen, not to reflect temporal patterns found in natural settings, and not to reflect temporal patterns derived from theory, but rather to fit into the experimental hour, or to be consistent with the times used for the same experimental tasks in previous studies. For the most part, laboratory researchers in social psychology have not been interested enough in time to manipulate it as an important independent variable. But they generally have controlled time by holding time intervals constant, counterbalancing orders of presentation, and so forth. They have recognized that permitting time (especially task-performance times) to vary naturally (hence, perhaps widely) could introduce substantial "noise" into the experimental data. At the same time, the control over both order and time of occurrence of events potentially available in laboratory settings would make it possible to make very precise specifications of temporal intervals involved in hypothesized causal processes. It is therefore doubly to be regretted that so few laboratory experiments in social psychology give attention to the study of such temporal factors.

In both judgment studies and sample surveys, the responses being observed are elicited by the experimenter's questions or stimuli and are not responses to the ongoing dynamics of the behavior setting. In both strategies, temporal factors such as order of stimuli are usually carefully controlled. In judgment studies, sequence and timing of stimuli are sometimes controlled because they are of interest and sometimes counterbalanced because leaving them free to vary might introduce error into results. In sample surveys, order of questions is often held constant for convenience in reproducing the survey materials, as well as because of a generalized bias in favor of standardization. Although collection of data *takes time* in both of these strategies, whether or not the responses are produced in "real time" is not really an applicable question. The responses themselves are artificial; that is, they are creatures of the research situation and generally would not occur at all outside of the study situation. Hence, we cannot really determine whether or not they occurred in the time "natural" to them in real situations. Time is important in these strategies only as a property of the research study itself, in terms of exercising control over features of the research situation. In judgment studies, control and/or measurement of order of stimuli and response times is important; and in sample surveys, preventing the infusion of "irrelevant" or unmeasured outside factors by spreading data collection over too long a period of time is crucial.

For formal theories, talking about real time versus experimental time makes no sense. Time enters these theories only conceptually, insofar as time is an important substantive variable in the theory (an occasion far too infrequent in our view). However, time plays an unusual role in computer simulations. Again, no "actors behaving in context" (Runkel & McGrath, 1972) are involved. But, like the experimental simulation, computer simulations involve an attempt to mirror the dynamics of the system being simulated, and those system dynamics are likely to have important temporal features, including both order and interval relations among variables. The simulation operates in its own time frame (in "computer time", so to speak, usually much faster than real time or even most uses of experimental time). Fidelity of the simulation (one aspect of validity for that strategy) requires that those temporal order and interval *relations* within the system dynamics *be preserved in the simulation*—though not necessarily in a form directly observable during a run of the simulation.

Thus, the strategies differ among themselves considerably in the way time is treated. Some operate in real time, some in an experimental time. Some attempt to make time irrelevant to the data. Some reflect time only in symbolic form. And all of these time differences play into the logic of causal inference that was discussed earlier in this chapter. If causal inference requires specification of an order of events, and if causal explanation requires specification of a time interval for the operation of causal processes, then it does make a difference how time is treated in our research settings. Experimental time is not the same as real time. If an experiment is intended to be a representation of a generic class of real-world systems, concocted in order to study analogues of real-world processes, then it is essential that the "experimental time" used in that analogue be a faithful representation of time as it operates within those real-world processes. Almost no real-world system processes operate in neat, one-link-of-the-chain-at-a-time fashion. Almost none of them operate so that the "stimulus" on one trial is independent of the response on the preceding trial (a characteristic that differentiates laboratory experiments, judgment studies, and sample surveys from field experiments, field studies, and experimental simulations). Almost no real-world processes operate in such a way that intervals between events are arbitrary (that is, do not depend on system forces) or of no consequence. And almost none of them operate so as to fit conveniently into an "experimental hour." Yet we seem to spend very little methodological effort trying to figure out *how best to transpose* between real time and experimental time, while preserving some of these essential temporal features of the system process that we wish to understand.

TEMPORAL FACTORS IN VALIDITY OF STUDY DESIGNS

"Research design" refers to the sets of choices the researcher makes in planning the treatments and observations that will be included in a study. One central concern in developing such a research plan is to make sure the design will permit the drawing of valid conclusions about causal relations. No design is perfect. Yet some are open to more, and more serious, threats to the validity of causal inferences than others.

In general, threats to the validity of a study represent plausible alternative hypotheses that rival the hypotheses under study as potential explanations for the relations found in the study. In other words, they represent alternative ways to account for the evidence of the study without invoking the cause–effect relation contained in the investigator's hypotheses. Many of these threats to validity of a study are temporal in nature; and many of the causes and corrections for these threats are also temporal in nature. These will be discussed in latter parts of this section of the chapter under the headings "internal validity" and "external validity," but before moving to that discussion, it is worth considering some general features of study designs and of the temporal patterns they involve.

TIME AND STUDY DESIGNS

The most primitive study design is the pattern that Campbell and Stanley (1966) refer to as the "one-shot design" and regard euphemistically as a "pre-experimental" design rather than a true experiment. This design calls for a single group of cases to be observed after they have all received a specific treatment. Even here, the temporal order required for causal interpretation is preserved. However, since knowledge is knowledge of differences, we cannot interpret such an effect without some other basis for comparison.

One way to get such a comparison basis would be to add a set of "pretest" observations that are obtained before the experimental treatment. The pretest observations must precede both the treatment and the posttest observations in time. The difference between the pretest and the posttest observations constitute some comparison leverage for interpreting the effect of the treatment. This second design is also fraught with flaws; it is also one of Campbell and Stanley's "pre-experimental" designs. A number of those flaws are reflected in threats to validity that have a temporal form. For example, since this design gets its comparison leverage by comparing two sets of observations that bracket the experimental treatment in time, that same temporal interval makes room for the entry of any of a number of time-related threats to validity. (Some of these, the effects of history, effects of maturation, and so forth, will be discussed in the next part of this section.)

Since this chapter is about temporal factors and not about research design, let us assume that an even more powerful design is used, one that employs not only a pre and post comparison but also comparisons between the experimental group and one or more control groups that did not receive any experimental treatment. Let us further assume that the designs to be discussed are all of the "true experiment" category, because they make use of a random procedure to allocate cases to the different comparison groups. (Excellent discussions of problems involving use of nonrandomized designs may be found in a number of sources, including Campbell & Stanley, 1966; Cook & Campbell, 1979; Runkel & McGrath, 1972.)

Adding a second comparison group that does not receive the experimental treatment strengthens the ability to draw valid causal inferences from the design since it allows for a baseline comparison against which some of the temporally based threats can be evaluated. In such a "pretest, posttest, control group" design, there is an added set of temporal relations involved in the comparisons. For both groups, the pretest precedes the posttest in time. For the experimental group, the treatment follows the pretest but precedes the posttest. So the pre to post time interval defined for the control group is divided into two intervals for the experimental group: a pretest to treatment interval, and a treatment to posttest interval. Recalling what was said in the preceding section of this chapter about the need to specify the time intervals involved in our causal interpretations, it is clear that those problems are made more complex as we draw upon more complex study designs.

Furthermore, in the idealized design, the pretest observations for both groups ought to be made simultaneously, and the posttest observations for both groups also should be made at the same time. If this simultaneity is not achieved, some events extraneous to the causal interpretation being explored may sneak into the time period for one set of observations and not for the other. The causal interpretation that is intended in the plan is thereby confounded. In practice, of course, observations of all of a relatively large number of cases cannot be done "simultaneously." Good experimental practice requires that a kind of cross-sectional simultaneity be preserved by insuring that equal numbers of (randomly chosen) experimental and control cases are premeasured or postmeasured at any one observation session, even though complete data collection may extend over many sessions and many days or months! Of course, if data collection extends over very long periods of time, even if such cross-sectional simultaneity is preserved, still other temporal problems may arise. "Outside" events (that we will call "history" in the next part of this section) and "inside" events (that we will later call "maturation") may occur. And although the comparison of experimental and no-treatment control groups will help discern the effects of history and maturation, that comparison won't be of much help if history or maturation (or other time-based) effects *interact with* the experimental treatment. Furthermore, if the data collection goes on too long, subjects in later sessions will almost certainly be aware of what was going on in both experimental and control conditions in the early sessions. (The phrasing here is in terms of laboratory studies; but this problem is at least as virulent in field settings, where it is often virtually impossible to keep as-yet-unstudied potential participants naive as to the study operations.)

We need to be concerned not only with the temporal order of events—pretest, treatment or no treatment, posttest—but also with the time intervals involved. If causal processes take time, and if there cannot be causal action at a temporal distance, then to really explain the differential flow of causal events in experimental versus control groups between the premeasurement and the postmeasurement of the effect, we need to explore these time intervals as well as their order. Specifically, we need to find out how long the treatment-to-posttest interval needs to be: (1) to allow enough time for the causal processes to operate to their fullest; while (2) not allowing so much time that some of it is "empty" of the operation of the causal processes; or (3) so much time that some other system forces have begun to operate so as to counter the causal forces under study; or (4) so much time that the effects of the cause have begun to wane. We need to pick the time intervals we impose, between pre and post observations and between treatment and post observations, just as carefully as we pick the concepts that are to be studied and the values of those concepts that are to be reflected in our experimental treatments, if we intend to make inferences about causal processes that are operating between the purported cause and the alleged effect.

All of these factors are of concern even if the causal processes involved produce monotonic and linear effects, as most of our theories assume. If the effect is actually cyclical, then none of the designs discussed thus far—and, indeed, none of the "true experimental" designs outlined by Campbell and Stanley—would be adequate to assess it. A design that is adequate to assess a cyclical effect requires not only a very careful theory involving postulates about the time course of the causal process, but also a design that includes measurement of the effects on a series of occasions carefully distributed over time. Such time series designs, developed for assessing treatment effects in situations in which a randomly allocated control group is not feasible (what Campbell and Stanley refer to as "quasi-experimental" designs), can be adapted to help identify possible cyclicality in causal processes.

Time series designs involve a series of observations distributed systematically across a relatively long time span, with an experimental treatment inserted at one or more spots within the series of observations. For example, we might take measures of production in a work organization every week. After 5 weeks, we might insert an experimental treatment (call it *A*). Then, after ten weeks we might remove Treatment *A* (if it were that kind of thing), and after 5 more weeks we might impose Treatment *B*. And so forth. We might or might not have a second factory, or a second department of the same factory, from which we gathered production data throughout the same period but made no interventions. Taking for granted many other design requirements for the moment, with such a design we could identify a cause–effect relation even if it were cyclical in time—*provided the interval was not smaller than a week, nor longer than the duration of the study, nor highly irregular in its variations.* But, of course, the very design complexity that makes it possible to do so opens the door for many other potential design threats, some of them temporal. Furthermore, if the time interval involved in our observations is based on administrative convenience (e.g., production records once a week) rather than on logical or theoretical considerations, even the complex and sophisticated forms of design will not help much in specifying the time course of causal processes. (If we had cyclical trends in productivity, as postulated in the above example, they certainly are as likely to occur within the day, or over months or seasons, as to occur on a week to week basis as the example would require.)

One form of such time series designs is called "longitudinal" designs. Many social scientists, especially those interested in studying social change, have called for more use of such longitudinal studies to assess long-run effects. But they too have some major weaknesses (see, Kulka, 1982). Complex designs involving combinations of longitudinal and cross-sectional comparisons are needed to separate out the historical (secular), the maturational (developmental), and the generational (cohort) effects that are all inevitably involved in the operation of long-run social change processes.

Within the study of social change there is the further problem of assessing stability and change over time in both the substantive variables of interest and in the instruments by which they will be measured. In most data-gathering situations, substantive change and unreliability of measures are quite intertwined and inseparable. The investigator must assume one of them is not operating in order to assess the other. As with questions of unconfounding history, development, and cohort effects within change data, separating out effects of substantive change from effects of unreliability of measures requires complex time series designs that, in their very complexity, infuse still other temporal problems into the matter.

Social change is always a very special methodological problem for social psychology. On the one hand, as already noted, social change is part of the natural substantive concerns of the field, although it always appears in a form confounded with unreliability of measures. On the other hand, the very fact of social change has seemed to some (see Gergen, 1973) to be an indication of the *failure* of social psychology to establish lawful relations, rather than as one of the phenomena properly to be regarded as part of the field of study. This, of course, assumes that all lawful relations are eternal, invariant over time. That serious scholars in the field should work on such an (implicit) assumption is strong testimony, indeed, as to just how little attention we have given to consideration of temporal features of our field. Perhaps the fact of social change, as one aspect of social phenomena in general, would have come as less of a shock to the field if all of us had given more attention to temporal aspects of our methodology in the past.

TEMPORAL FACTORS IN INTERNAL VALIDITY

The previous section hinted at some of the validity issues associated with temporal features of research strategies and study designs. For example, additional validity problems may arise when there are very long temporal intervals between the events that are the putative causes and effects, as well as when the data-collection period extends over a very long time. Here, we will take up those and other temporal issues as they relate to the internal validity of a study.

Earlier, we commented on the cultural custom of preferring causal interpretations in which the cause and effect are close together in time (and space). We also noted that Hume regarded such temporal or spatial contiguity as the only "rational" (albeit logically incorrect) basis for inferring a necessary connection between a cause and an effect. We also noted that this preference for temporal contiguity rests in part on appreciation of the fact that the longer the temporal interval between the cause and effect of interest is, the more chance there is for intervening events to occur between the cause and the effect. Such intervening events can either obscure or enhance the cause–effect relation being studied, or present the investigator with a spurious relation that is mistaken for the one being studied.

Consider an example. A little boy hits a little girl. She drops her skateboard. It rolls off the porch and trips a person on the sidewalk. That person falls into the street in front of an oncoming car. That car swerves to avoid the fallen person, and thereupon hits a second, parked car. What does it mean to draw the causal inference that the parked car was hit because the little boy hit the little girl? The two events—putative cause and putative effect of that cause—are separated in time, and also in functional steps or links in the logical chain. During that time, several other relevant events occurred: the dropping of the skateboard, the pedestrian tripping, the swerving of the first car. Our causal inference, that the hitting of the parked car was caused by the hitting of the little girl, does not really seem to be sound because so many things took place in the interval between them. The temporal interval is really not so large—perhaps a matter of seconds or a minute between cause and consequence—but the *logical* interval is many–stepped.

What is critical to our inference is not length of time as such, but rather the extent to which other factors could have played an instigating role. The size of the time interval is simply the size of the window through which those other factors could have entered the situation. Those factors could be within the chain we have listed (e.g., the falling skateboard, the tripped person, the swerving of the oncoming car). Or, they could be other factors in the situation, not yet brought into the picture. For example, if it turned out that the brakes or steering of the moving car were faulty, or that the little girl threw the skateboard, or that the falling person was drunk, those new facts might cloud our causal conclusion—although they would not alter the temporal contiguity of the relevant factors very much. Or, other factors could lie in still earlier antecedant conditions (e.g., if the boy's action was in response to earlier teasing by the little girl) and this, too, might alter our interpretation of the causal processes involved.

Without belaboring this example any further, we can note that all of these considerations confound the temporal and the logical relations involved in the case. We can have logical complexity with temporal contiguity; or logical simplicity with temporal distance; or the other combinations of the two. And although we tend to assign temporal contiguity a key role in our willingness to make causal inferences, it may well be the logical contiguity that is the more telling feature of such situations. (As a final note on this example, if this were a legal case, the judge would have to rule partly on the basis of "foreseeable consequences." That is, the little boy would be assigned causal responsibility only if the little boy [or any "reasonable man (sic)"] could foresee that his action [hitting the girl] would result in the chain of events leading to the hitting of the parked car. This, also, gives logical directness a more prominent role than literal temporal contiguity.)

The "sleeper effect" is another example, perhaps more apt. A persuasive message, delivered at time 1 from a particular source, is the presumed cause of attitude change at time 2, perhaps several months later. The validity of this inference about the cause–effect relation is threatened because many different events *could have* occurred in the interval to produce the attitude change. The person may have been exposed to other persuasive messages; or may have been prompted to discuss the issue with friends whose views helped produce the attitude change; or may simply have been acclimated to the view expressed in the initial communication, hence become more receptive to it when it appeared in other messages. Each of these possible intervening events either weakens or makes more complex the causal linkage between the original message and the ultimate attitude change.

Earlier, we mentioned that strong designs often use extra comparison groups in order to rule out the effects of intervening events other than the experimental treatment(s) that might have occurred between pretest and posttest observations. Campbell and colleagues (Campbell & Stanley, 1966; Cook & Campbell, 1979) call these potential intervening events "threats to internal validity," and have identified seven major classes of them: history, maturation, testing (or reactivity), instrument decay (or, more generally, instrument change), regression to the mean, selection, and mortality. All seven of these are profoundly temporal in character and in cause.

"History" refers to the fact that the actor's behavior can be affected by other events, besides the experimental treatment(s), that could have occurred between pretest and posttest. Such outside events can produce an effect like the one being studied, or obscure the observation of such an effect. Such events could arise in the environment surrounding the whole study, or just in the environment of the experimental group (Cook and Campbell refer to the latter case as being "local history" and of having its effect in the form of an interaction of history and experimental treatment). As the interval between treatment and post observation increases, so does the opportunity for the operation of such outside events.

"Maturation" refers to changes within the actors themselves, changes that occur during the passage of time and that are independent of the occurrence of the experimental treatment. These internal events, developments within the social systems under study, also can either enhance, or obscure, or display a spurious form of, the cause–effect relation under study. Here, too, as more time passes (between pretest and posttest), more maturational change takes place.

To show how such effects are linked to the temporal interval, let us consider an example that approaches a *reducto ad absurdum* case. Suppose we obtained a premeasure of something like "dancing grace" of a kindergarten class, then waited until those same pupils were in grade 6 to impose a dancing class as an experimental treatment (for a randomly assigned half of them), then waited again until their senior year to obtain a follow-up measure of "dancing grace" on both experimental and control groups. Suppose, too, that there was a significant difference between the means of the two groups. It is unlikely that anyone would be very willing to credit the obtained systematic difference in dancing grace between the two groups of seniors solely or even mainly to that sixth-grade dancing class. We could spin out all sorts of ways in which such an intervention could have had a contributing effect, in interaction with other events, earlier and later. And we would have to face squarely the possibility that our non-chance finding was, indeed, obtained by chance. But above all, we would want to consider the possibility that other factors—not known to or measured by us—had occurred and had done so in a nonrandom pattern across the two groups of students. Remember that when we talk about "all other things equal" between control and experimental groups, we always implicitly have the caveat, " . . . insofar as we know . . ." And the 12 years from K to senior, and even the 6 years from sixth grade to senior, is a long time within which many of those "other things" could have taken place, unbeknownst to us. The duration of the temporal interval from pretest to posttest is an index of how wide open the temporal window was through which these extraneous effects could have entered.

"Testing" or reactivity effects refer to changes that occur in an actor's behavior because the process of measurement itself sensitizes the actor to his or her own behavior. It denotes effects at the end of the measurement interval that were unintentionally produced by what was done during the interval. The time interval between premeasure and postmeasure can interact with such testing effects, in any of several ways. As the time interval increases, the sensitization due to testing may increase or may fade. But even if the latter takes place, making testing a less competitive rival hypothesis, the increase in interval opens wider the window of time through which history and maturational effects may enter. Besides, the intended effects of the experimental treatment, the study of which is the underlying purpose of all of this activity, may also fade during such an extended time interval.

"Instrument decay," or the more general term "instrument change," refers to the effects that ensue when a measurement device changes calibration during the data-collection period. For physical instruments (e.g., mechanical or electronic devices), extended use increases the chances for parts to break or wear out or rust. For human instruments (as in observers or interviewers), either short but full intervals, or long intervals whether full or empty, may have adverse effects on instrument performance: fatigue, boredom, forgetting, new learning, and above all, shifts in motivation, all may undercut the reliability and validity of human judgments involved in research measurements.

Both "regression to the mean" and "selection" are threats to validity that arise because the fundamental experimental principle of randomization has been ignored. The former refers to shifts in distributions of scores of subjects, selected into extreme groups on the basis of a pretest, when they are subsequently retested. It is a statistical artifact, not a logical one. Although there is a specific temporal pattern involved in this validity threat, it is hard to make a generalization about whether the threat is aggravated as the interval between testings is increased.

"Selection" refers to the assignment of actors to treatment conditions on any basis other than random allocation from a common pool. Such selection increases the chances that the comparison groups will differ in ways not related to the experimental treatment and that such differences will be mistaken for the causal effects being studied. Selection, too, does not in general relate to temporal differences, except that longer time intervals imply longer times in which any factors selected can operate to make comparison groups noncomparable. The longer the time, the wider the window through which effects of selection can enter.

Finally, "mortality" or subject attrition refers to effects that can accrue when some of the actors who participated at the first measurement drop out of the study before the final measurement takes place. This may affect the distribution of characteristics in the treatment groups, and do so differentially—that is, it may undo the effects achieved by random allocation. Attrition also may interact with the treatment itself, making the interpretation problem more serious. When a study extends beyond a single session, there is likely to be some attrition; and the longer it extends, the more attrition there is likely to be. So the scope of the problem is directly linked to time, and the seriousness of the problem depends on sampling, design, measurement, and other considerations.

Thus, most of these threats to internal validity, that is, threats to sound causal interpretation of experimental results, contain crucial temporal features and can be aggravated by temporal features of the study design. The trick, for the investigator, is to arrange the temporal order relations and intervals among comparison groups and measurement occasions so as to maximize the chances of detecting the hypothesized effect while at the same time minimizing the threats to a valid interpretation of that effect as having arisen from the hypothesized cause.

TEMPORAL FACTORS IN EXTERNAL VALIDITY

Many researchers seem to operate under the assumption that one period of time is the same as any other. This may be a shaky assumption on a number of levels. Phenomenologically, most people experience time (at least some of the time!) as epochal, as a phasic flow rather than as a smooth linear progression, in which different periods of time may be qualitatively different from one another. At another level, human life is filled with cycles and rhythms, from diurnal cycles of activity and temperature variations to seasonal cycles that bring with them variations in human activities, moods, and interests as well as differences in weather. At still another level, there are life stage variations and generational differences that alter both activities and attitudes. It is clear that we need to take into account these nonhomogeneous features of time as experienced if we hope to understand how the substantive phenomena of our field are or are not stable and generalizable over time.

Cohort differences, which sometimes are also generational differences, can be viewed in any of several ways. Some investigators have capitalized on such differences as the route by which social change can be studied. Others have interpreted them as evidence of instability of our substantive findings over time, hence as evidence of our inability to establish lawful and universal relations among concepts of interest in our studies. Gergen (1973), for instance, has claimed that we may only be able to document historical relations rather than "discover" real or basic ones. We have already made one comment on this argument—noting that it assumes, incorrectly, that "lawful" is synonymous with "eternal." We make the further comment that the Gergen criticism ought to be taken seriously; but that it ought to be used to draw attention to the need for making generalization over time a keystone within our efforts to establish the external validity of our research findings.

Up until now, such an emphasis on generalization over time has certainly not been a central feature of efforts toward establishing external validity. There has been surprisingly little effort devoted to external validity in any case, and most of that effort has focused on generalization over populations. Here, as in other aspects of our field (and of our culture) we have tended to treat time as a "merely": merely a medium within which events take place; merely a dimension of the space–time continuum; merely an abstract parameter that we can use to locate and track people and events; and the like.

We could argue that such cavalier treatment of such an important chunk of human experience is misleading. It is rather like saying that we should not bother to study human individuals because they are "merely" the location of certain consequences; merely the agents of many sorts of actions; merely the sources of most of the important stimulation; merely the carriers of the technological and social institutions of the culture. While that set of statements about individuals might be literally true, just as the statements about time are, preceding each of them with the pejorative "merely" is certainly misleading in both cases.

Perhaps one reason why we have given time so little attention, either as a substantive variable or in our efforts to establish the external validity of our findings, is, ironically, because people in our culture tend to be impatient, to be in a hurry. To study generational effects *in a way that separates out historical, developmental, and cohort effects,* takes at least several generations. To do cross-sectional comparisons across generations takes much less time. To study static conditions is easier still, in part because it is quicker. *To study time takes time* (and, in our culture, time is scarce, hence valuable, hence not to be "wasted").

Temporal Factors at the Method or Operational Level

Temporal factors also pervade our methodology at the operational level. Time is a crucial part of the methods by which we measure, manipulate, and control the variables that we study. Time is crucial to the logic by which we assess reliability. Many of our independent variable manipulations involve temporal order or interval. Many of our dependent variables are measures in terms of some temporal parameters (frequency, rate, etc.). And many of those measures involve critical temporal features (leads, lags) in their measurement. Here, too, we have given temporal matters much less attention than their importance would seem to merit.

Social and behavioral sciences have leaned on strong assumptions about stability and linearity of phenomena over time to strengthen many aspects of their logic of method. Such assumptions about time also underlie the logic by which we assess the quality (that is, the reliability and validity) of our measures and concepts.

The logical operations for assessing reliability inevitably confound at least three kinds of changes over time: (1) real change versus temporal invariance of the phenomena: (2) fluctuations of the phenomena over time that represent only minor variations of essentially stable phenomena; and (3) unreliability in the measures of the phenomena even though the phenomena themselves are stable over time. Furthermore, various techniques that are used to deal with such confounding, and with the problem of cause–effect intervals as well, rely heavily on the idea that anything that goes on over time does so as some regular and monotonic, or even linear, function of time. So, for example, when we compare changes between two trials that were a certain temporal distance apart, with changes between two other trials that were much further apart, we are apt to expect proportionality. That is, we assume that the relative sizes of the changes in our measures, in relation to the intertrial intervals, reflect directly the temporal course of the change process involved. It is *as if* we expected time to map isomorphically to all other measurement scales, and as if we assumed that the ratio (or interval) properties of our time measure "rubbed off" on those other measures. That would be true only if all change processes acted in a smooth, monotonic if not linear fashion. However, many processes operate in cyclical, or oscillatory, or rhythmic fashion, violating the assumptions of the interpretive logic underlying those change comparisons.

The concept of reliability, per se, involves a crucial temporal feature. The underlying logic of reliability is that we compare *two simultaneous but experimentally independent applications of the same measuring instrument to the same objects or phe-*

nomena to be measured. This is, of course, impossible to realize in practice. So, all methods for assessing the reliability of measurements proceed by relaxing one or another of the constraints in that definition. Some, such as test–retest procedures, set aside the simultaneity assumption (and try, in various ways, to wrestle with the experimentally independent assumption). Others, such as alternate forms and split half procedures, set aside the assumption that it is the very *same* instrument that is being used in the two independent measurements.

The test–retest approach assumes that the variable being measured is *constant over time*, both in the real change sense and in the transitory fluctuation sense. Therefore, if there are any differences between the first and the second measurements, those differences are attributed to *unreliability (instability) of the measure of the variable.* Note that many of the threats to validity that we have already discussed—history, maturation, testing, and the like—may operate within the interval between the two testing applications. The shorter the interval between the two testing occasions, the less tenable is the assumption that the two measurements were experimentally independent. (Another way to look at this effect is to say that the shorter the time, the more testing or reactivity effects may come into play.) The longer the interval between the two testing occasions, the more room there is (i.e., the wider the temporal window) for the operation of such other factors as history, maturation, and the like, that can pose threats to the "internal validity" of the reliability assessment activities.

We put internal validity in quotation marks in the preceding sentence to make a point. Operations for establishing the reliability of a test or other measure is one case of a research design. It is curious that such reliability testing is seldom discussed in our literature as involving a study design, and as therefore being potentially vulnerable to all of the threats to internal validity that beset other study designs. If it were treated more as a kind of research design, we would probably notice that such reliability-testing study designs are almost always pre-experimental, seldom true experiments; that they seldom include relevant comparison groups (knowledge of reliability is also knowledge of potential differences); and that both the sampling and the allocation procedures involved are seldom made explicit.

Manipulation of independent variables, putative causes, often involve temporal parameters directly. Sometimes frequency, rate, and/or duration of stimuli are critical features of the independent variable. Sometimes manipulanda involve anticipation intervals, warning times, and the like. The study procedures within which the manipulanda are embedded also contain some critical temporal features: questions of sequence of stimuli, order of presentation, and the like. These arrangements are mostly built on the assumption that changes in the behavioral processes of interest are not only monotonic but linear, and that the processes somehow involve ratio scales with respect to time. While every experiment deals with and resolves all of these issues, they are seldom regarded as important methodological matters. But many of these time-based features of experimental manipulations rest on important assumptions about the nature of the phenomena being studied and carry important consequences for the information contained in the study.

Most often, decisions about the temporal unit of analysis, about intervals within the experimental procedures, and about order relations among conditions are made on the basis of convention. If a certain working time interval was used for a task in the past, it will most likely be used in the future for the same task. If an effect was supposed to have occurred in a previous study after a 15-minute delay, a 15-minute delay will probably be the only interval used in a subsequent study of the same effect. Standardization is an important principle of good research design, to be sure. But standardization is only one of a number of important principles, some conflicting with one another. The exclusive use of the *same* procedures in successive studies of a phenomena have some serious strategic consequences for our knowledge of that phenomena. McGrath,

Martin, and Kulka (1982) argue, for example, that following identical standardized procedures in all studies on a given topic has the effect of limiting the potential information gain of each new study. When we note that, more often than not, these conventional choices were made, in the first place, for the convenience of fitting into an experimental hour, it is clear why such studies yield little information bearing on the temporal course of causal processes.

Another time-related principle of good experimentation that also has some negative side effects is counterbalancing of order of presentation of stimuli or conditions. While counterbalancing prevents such order relations from being confounded with the stimulus conditions under study, it also prevents investigation of some potentially interesting and important features of the phenomena under study.

One reason why temporal factors are so pervasive in our experimental treatments is the strong influence of logical positivism and behaviorism within our field. Time is a very measurable property of events. Furthermore, using objective or clock time does not seem to require any metaphysical analysis or the postulating of any theoretical concepts. Behaviorists not only make use of rates and frequencies in their experimental treatments, but they also consider the distribution of events within intervals as important. Fixed and variable reinforcement ratios and the use of interval or ratio reinforcement schedules are all part of the standard set of operational definitions of many behavioristic studies. All of these, of course, are temporal concepts. Each type of reinforcement schedule is associated with different patterns of response—near step functions, scalloped shaped, and so forth—over time.

TIME AND EXPERIMENTAL EFFECTS

Many of our measures of effects also contain important temporal features. Here, too, there is a strong influence of the behaviorists, again probably in large part because of the ease of making time measurements that appear not to have any problems of reliability, validity, and the like. Many dependent variables involve rates or frequencies of responding, latencies or reaction times for a response, and so forth.

Rate is a record of number of some kind of occurrence per some predetermined unit of time. Frequency and rate are, arithmetically, interchangeable. What such measures ignore is the distribution of events throughout the interval. It is perhaps no accident that some of the strongest (that is, more repeatable) findings in our field are the behaviorist's relations between reinforcement schedules and cumulative amount and pattern of response in relation to learning, extinction, and other processes.

TEMPORAL ASPECTS OF INFERRED PROCESSES

Many of the time-based techniques used in experimental psychology are being applied in social psychology to the study of social memory and information processing. Use of these measures requires a panel of strong assumptions about the mappings of temporal factors within cognitive structures and processes. In this work, reaction times or response latencies are taken to be indicators of stimulus difficulty and as indicators of layers or distances within internal cognitive structures, as well as evidences of performance effectiveness (i.e., speed). Moreover, use of these measures rests on the assumptions that time intervals in the millisecond range reflect meaningful differences in cognitive processes, and that changes in the relevant behavioral processes map not only monotonically, but strictly linearly, to important differences in cognitive structures. Furthermore, this body of work involves the additional implicit assumptions that all processes take some finite amount of time, that the parts are carried out in temporal sequence rather than all at the same time, and that all cognitive processes or subprocesses are always carried out in the *minimum possible time*—else why would "quicker" mean "structurally or organizationally closer"? Finally, this work ultimately assumes that the behavior processes involved (time to recall or recognize) can somehow be mapped to the time course of various neurological processes as reflected in brain activity.

At the same time, workers in that same content area make use of time concepts in a much cruder fashion when they study how delays affect the recall of cognitive materials, and how such delays alter memory after priming has taken place. There is virtually no specification in that body of work about how long it takes for such processes to work. Delay intervals seem to be set far more on the basis of experimental convenience than on the basis of any attempt to reckon with the temporal parameters of the processes under study. The postdelay measurement is likely to be carried out toward the end of the experimental hour, at the same time the next day or 2 days later, or at the same time 1 week later—perhaps reflecting class-schedule patterns more than the temporal processes being studied.

Such cavalier treatment of time intervals is also true in the attitude-change area. Laboratory studies of attitude change often seem to expect attitudes—usually defined as relatively stable patterns—nevertheless to change within the experimental hour (or if not by then, perhaps by the same time tomorrow or next week!). Field studies of attitude change are much more likely to deal with relatively long intervals, months, years, or even decades. All that we have said about causal process intervals is applicable here as well. The longer the interval, the more the change reflects many things in addition to the events of the study, and such studies may indeed show no change when real change has taken place—and faded or been counteracted in the interim. The shorter the interval, the more the change may reflect only the reactivity effects of the research operations themselves.

Indeed, both studies of delays in cognitive processing and studies of attitude change are but special cases of the more general problem: *How to set the time interval between events of interest and measured consequences so that it is more or less exactly filled with the operation of some plausible and definite change or causal process.* That problem faces any investigator who intends to conduct an experiment on *any* topic. Designs always involve the measurement of presumed effects at some specifiable time after the deliberate manipulation, or natural occurrence, of presumed causes. Choosing that time interval, or rationalizing the use of some time interval, necessarily entails spinning out a theory of the temporal course of the processes involved whether or not the investigator formulates that theory explicitly and whether or not he or she wants to explore those temporal features of the phenomena.

Time and the Measurement of Behavior

TEMPORAL FEATURES OF CLASSES OF MEASURES

Many measures have special temporal properties or constraints directly involved in their use. These need to be reckoned with in research planning and analysis, and, too often, are overlooked. For example: in stress research, one class of measures, generally accepted as useful indexes of reaction to some stressor, are on-line, real-time physiological measures such as galvanic skin response (GSR), pulse rate, respiratory rate, and the like. These tend to be labile measures, requiring the establishment of baseline levels and the readjustment of running levels for adaptations during extended periods of data collection. In interpretation of such measures, specific values at specific short periods of time are usually accredited to specific stimuli or conditions occurring immediately prior to the moment of measurement.

In contrast, another group of measures, also usually regarded as good measures of reaction to stressors, are those assessing the levels of various constituents of blood and urine. These cannot be done on-line. Rather, the researcher must wait a substantial time (a matter of hours) after the putative causal events in order for the constituents of interest to build up to measurable levels. On the one hand, they avoid some of the data-quality problems associated with labile measures observed on-line in real time. They yield indexes that are much less labile, ephemeral, and transitory than the GSR-type measures. But at the same time, they do not permit isolation of the effects of any one stress event, but rather assess the net effects of all events that occurred within the time period of the study.

Still a third class of measures often used in stress research are self-reports, such as adjective checklists or rating scales. These are virtually time-independent, insofar as administration of them is concerned. They can be used on-line, but more often are used in retrospect, either immediately or after a delay. They can be used in anticipation of stress events not yet experienced—and even in anticipation of hypothetical stress events that will never be experienced. This enormous temporal flexibility is paid for at a high cost in reactivity, and in other potential validity problems.

Suppose you obtained a battery of measures of stress effects containing some of each of these classes (e.g., GSR, a blood sample, and a self-report), and then analyzed the results so as to ask the triangulation or convergent validity question. It is likely that they would show little convergence, simply because of their diversity on temporal characteristics, quite apart from the question of whether or not any one of them is a valid measure of stress or whether stress is a valid and useful concept.

These problems extend far beyond stress research. Indeed, such temporal features are characteristic of certain classes of measures. Self-reports are versatile with respect to the temporal features of their use; they can be used during, immediately after, with a delay, in anticipation, or in relation to, hypothetical but nonoccurring events. But that very temporal flexibility brings with it threats to validity. A short time interval courts reactivity effects. A long interval courts faulty or biased memory of the event. On-line observations may avoid some of the problems of temporal interval, but do so at a high cost in personnel, equipment, and training effort needed to obtain high-quality data in a labile situation. Archival records, presumably recorded without research reactivity, may nevertheless suffer from what might be called administrative reactivity (distortions in what is recorded, and how, as a function of ongoing forces in the system whose behavior is being examined). Furthermore, such threats of potential selective recording and selective survival increase with the length of time interval between recording and use. Trace measures, of which the GSR is an example, also avoid problems of reactivity, because they are by definition accretions or erosions made by the behavior itself unbeknownst to the actors involved. But they are, at the same time, entirely opaque with respect to the time intervals involved: time since the trace was recorded, time process involved in the laying down of the record, and so forth.

Measures of *temporal duration* have been used to assess a wide range of variables in social-psychological research. "Duration" refers to the temporal interval between the onset and the offset of some event. Time durations are relatively easy to assess, and equipment to measure them accurately, even for extremely small time units (e.g., milliseconds), is portable and easily concealed. Most people wear watches, and the sight of someone checking their timepiece does not necessarily arouse undue suspicion. Thus, durations can be measured fairly unobtrusively (e.g., Webb, Campbell, Schwartz, Sechrest, & Grove, 1981).

Duration has been used, for example, to assess the degree of interest in or attraction to certain objects, products, or other people. The time spent working on a task can be taken as a measure of intrinsic interest in the task. Time taken to complete a task has also been used to indicate the intrinsic interest of a distracting stimulus. The duration of mutual gaze has been used as an indicator of interpersonal attraction, and also as an indicator of truthfulness or trustworthiness in a speaker. Finally, time durations have been used to assess the amount of cognitive processing involved in certain tasks (e.g., reaction times in cognitive tasks).

All classes of measures tend to have characteristic and differing temporal properties, and sensible interpretation of data resulting from their use requires that these be taken into account. Yet, how little we have thought and written about these matters, either in our reports of substantive efforts, such as in stress research, or in our methodological literature. These features of method, and many others not discussed in this chapter for lack of space, are crucial temporal features of our research process. We cannot make them go away; we can (and have, for the most part) ignored them. But as in all other instances in which we ignore serious methodological issues, those issues often become the undoing of our methods in ways not always easy to identify. So it is, we believe, currently, in regard to temporal factors in many areas of social psychology.

Concluding Comments

This chapter began with a discussion of how temporal matters play a central role in the logic of our methods. Crucial to the logic of method is the idea of an order relation between cause and effect, antecedent and consequent. Also crucial to our causal logic is the idea of a time interval during which a (causal) process operates. We have argued that a careful specification of the temporal interval between cause and effect is a necessary condition for strong inferences about the processes that have occurred. A mapping of the temporal course of the processes under study should be an integral part of the formulation of any theory about those processes.

We have also argued that time is an important consideration in our choice of research strategies and designs. Different experimental strategies carry with them different assumptions about the real-time operation of the processes under study. All too often processes are allowed to unfold in a time frame that reflects convenience within the experimental hour rather than in a time frame that reflects the operation of those processes in their natural settings.

Our choice of experimental design for research often reflects our desire to control for threats to the drawing of valid causal conclusions. Many of those threats are temporal in nature. Yet we often ignore the temporal considerations of those designs—issues of temporal ordering, simultaneity, temporal intervals, and the like—that increase in complexity as the sophistication of our designs increase.

Finally, we discussed the ubiquitousness of time factors within our dependent variable measures and our manipulations of independent variables. This pervasive use comes mainly, we would argue, because time is very easy to measure and time intervals are very easy to administer as manipulanda. However, these operations make many strong assumptions about the mapping of these time measurements to the processes under consideration, often including assumptions of linearity and monotonicity of the processes with respect to time. Those assumptions may not accurately reflect the states of nature that are under investigation.

There are, therefore, temporal considerations underlying the very fabric of our logic-of-method. But often, these temporal issues are ignored or dealt with in rather arbitrary ways. We must, therefore, look carefully at the meanings of our accumulated research findings in all areas of the field, whether or not the substance of those findings has to do with temporal matters. Many of our findings have been based on strong time order and time interval logic, without our studies having given any particular attention or thought to the time intervals used in them. We must give more time to time, even if we are not interested in studying temporal factors per se, in order to meet the requirements of our methods.

C H A P T E R 7

Toward a Social Psychology of Time

This book is built on the premise that it is both desirable and possible to develop an area of study that would provide a "social psychology of time." In the first chapter of the book, we argued that temporal factors were important within, and had not been adequately investigated by, social psychology and some related areas of study. In the intervening chapters, we have tried to do two main things:

1. To raise the readers' consciousness, so to speak, about how fundamental and pervasive temporal factors are within the conceptual, substantive, and methodological domains of our field. We have tried to do so by raising many issues regarding temporal matters, issues we thought both interesting and important.
2. To give readers a general picture of the kinds of theoretical and empirical work that can be done on these

temporal issues. We have tried to do so by reviewing research in key topical areas that deals with those temporal issues. Some of that review draws on our own work, conceptual and empirical; most of it draws on the work of other researchers/scholars in the field.

We have not tried to be exhaustive in either of those two tasks. There are many other interesting and important temporal questions that we have not raised. There are also other research efforts that deal with or bear upon important temporal topics that we did not review. We could not deal with all the questions or all the work, due to our own conceptual and scholarly limitations as well as to practical limitations of time and space. We regret what we have overlooked, but do not apologize for having to be selective in our coverage.

Above all, we want the book to help open up an area of study—the study of time at the social-psychological level. So, in our selection of material, we have been more interested in being provocative than in being definitive, more interested in pointing out heretofore unnoticed distinctions and connections than in treating any specific topical area thoroughly and systematically. To follow that strategy is to risk having readers feel they have been offered a profusion of scattered ideas purporting to be insights, but no thorough treatment of any of the topics covered.

In this final chapter, we will try to accomplish three goals. First, we will try to summarize what we think are the key ideas presented in various parts of the book, and the key "lessons to be learned" from that material. Second, we will try to lay out some definitions and formulations that may help us build a common language for talking about temporal factors, especially for talking quantitatively about them. Third, we will try to lay out some of the key research tasks that seem to us most promising as steps toward a social psychology of time.

SUMMARY: MAIN IDEAS OF THE BOOK

As we noted in Chapter 1, we can consider the material in the main chapters of this book as dealing with the impact of temporal factors in conceptual, substantive, and methodological aspects of our field. Chapters 2 and 3 deal, primarily, with conceptual matters. Chapters 4 and 5 deal mainly with substantive material. Chapter 6 deals with methodological considerations. We will review the main ideas offered in those chapters, and the "lessons" to be learned from them, in that same order of presentation.

MULTIPLE AND CONFLICTING CONCEPTIONS OF TIME

The material in Chapters 2 and 3 has to do with the plethora of ways in which we can conceptualize time. One key "lesson" to be learned from that material is that each of these conceptualizations carries with it a series of assumptions about the nature of events, and these assumptions constrain the ways in which we can understand the meanings of those events. Furthermore, many of the anomalies and paradoxes that have been noted in past studies of time can be interpreted as resulting from the unwitting juxtaposition of two or more such conflicting conceptions of time. We therefore need extra caution in dealing with temporal issues. We must try not to interpret results as important temporal phenomena when they may have arisen mainly from our own arbitrary use of some particular time perspective that may be inappropriate to the phenomena at hand. On the other hand, the availability of such multiple and conflicting conceptions of time offers us the opportunity to step outside of our own characteristic ways of looking at time and into alternative temporal paradigms. This can provide us with a way to conduct "thought experiments" on the implications of those alternative conceptions for the social-psychological phenomena in which we are interested.

RHYTHMS OF BEHAVIOR AND THEIR SOCIAL ENTRAINMENT

The material in Chapters 4 and 5 deals with the temporal patterning of behavior in social and organizational settings. It is a call to look at things more dynamically than we have done in the past. That material makes clear the need to study temporal patterns through time (that is, social process), rather than to study just their static outcomes. It also points to the pervasiveness of cyclical patterns, endogenous to individual and social behavior, and to a variety of ways in which those rhythms can become entrained or otherwise modified. Furthermore, the material in those chapters argues for the recognition that solutions to inherent temporal problems at one system level (e.g., by an organization) sometimes create parallel temporal problems at another system level (e.g., an individual member of that organization). Above all, that material shows, as did the material from Chapters 2 and 3, that taking different temporal perspectives can change the meanings we assign to events and can redefine "the problem." Finally, the material of those two chapters makes it clear that there are strong entrainment effects from the work situation, under normal as well as under unusual work-shift conditions, and that these can have important consequences for other aspects of life (and vice versa).

THE TEMPORAL LOGIC OF OUR RESEARCH METHOD

The material in Chapter 6 deals with the many ways in which temporal considerations play a part in our research methodology. It shows that many temporal issues underlie the logic of our research process, and often go unattended. The chief moral to be drawn from it is that, if we are to live up to the logical requirements of our methods, we must give much more attention to temporal matters than we have done to date. It is especially crucial that we begin to specify much more carefully not only the time order but also the time intervals between our putative causes and their alleged effects. Time intervals between cause and effect should be a matter of theory rather than experimental convenience.

FINAL COMMENTS

These and other key ideas, presented and implied in the earlier chapters of this book, seem to us to make a strong case at least for the importance of studying temporal factors at the social-psychological level, and perhaps for the desirability of developing a full-fledged social psychology of time. We believe that temporal factors permeate the field—in conceptual, substantive, and methodological domains. Furthermore, it seems to us that, not only can we advance the field of social psychology by giving more attention to these temporal factors, but we are definitely hindering its advance by failing to do so.

Perhaps one factor that has hindered the development of a social psychology of time is the lack of a common language for talking about temporal concepts and measures. In the next section of this chapter we offer some suggestions for such a common language.

Temporal Parameters: Some Terms for a Common Language for Measuring Time

We have already introduced a number of different conceptions of time (potentially, 256 such conceptions, although for practical purposes there are considerably fewer than that). We also have introduced a number of time frames within which the individual needs to be able to locate instants and events. Furthermore, we have referred to various aspects of time—rate, frequency, duration, rhythms, intervals, and so forth. Given this plethora of time conceptions, time frames, and other time terms, it seems worthwhile to try to lay out a set of terms that can provide a standard language for speaking of time, and especially for talking about time in quantitative terms. The task of this section is to formulate such a set of terms.

First, let us make certain *assumptions*:

1. Let us assume a time line, T, to which we will reference all temporal locations. We may as well assume one that takes the form of a Gregory Newton calendar-clock, with a set of distinguishable but adjacent points, $t_1, t_2, t_3, \ldots t_i, t_j \ldots t_n$, of arbitrarily small size but with no "space" between them. Let T extend infinitely in both directions from an arbitrary point, t_0. (An upper case italic T with subscript will be used

to refer to quantities of time. Lower case italic t with subscript will be used to refer to locations along the time line T.)

2. Let us assume a set of event classes, A, B, C, . . . N, with any given event being a member of one and only one class.

3. Let us assume a set of events of class A, A_1, A_2, A_3, . . . A_i, A_j, . . . A_n. We will also regard these as the occurrence of the same event, A, on different occasions, with the constraint that A_j does not precede A_i.

4. Let us further assume that an event, A_i, has two states: ON and OFF. We will use $A_{i_{ON}}$ to represent the time of onset of A_i. We will use $A_{i_{OFF}}$ to represent the time of offset of A_i. Similarly, we will use $A_{j_{ON}}$ for the time of onset of A_j, or the time of onset of a second occurrence of A_i; $A_{j_{OFF}}$ for the time of offset of A_j, or the time of offset of a second occurrence of A_i. All four of these points are expressed as a location, t_i, on T.

Upon these assumptions, let us now build the following *definitions*:

"Occurrence" of an event is when there is a change of state of that class of events, from OFF to ON.

"Recurrence" of an event is when there is a sequence of state changes of that class of events, from OFF to ON to OFF to ON.

"Duration" of an event, i, is the ON_i–OFF_i interval.

"Period" of recurrence of an event is the ON_i–OFF_i–ON_j interval, or simply the ON_i–ON_j interval. It cannot be negative, by definition. If it is zero, that is onset simultaneity.

"Interval" between occurrences of an event is the OFF_i–ON_j interval. It can be positive (a gap), negative (an overlap), or zero (continuity).

"Rhythm" is an ON_i–OFF_i–ON_j–OFF_j–ON_k–OFF_k . . . sequence with either: (a) equal intervals between successive ON–OFF–ON sequences (equal successive periods); or (b) recurring identical *sequences of intervals* between successive ON–OFF–ON sequences.

We can define some of those terms and some others more precisely (or more quantitatively) as follows:

"Location" of event A_i = t_i of onset of event A_i = $A_{i_{ON}}$.

"Duration" of event $A_i = D_i = A_{i_{OFF}} - A_{i_{ON}}$.

"Period" of recurrence of event $A_i = P_i = A_{j_{ON}} - A_{i_{ON}}$, $P > 0$. As P approaches zero, A_i becomes approximately equal to A_j (a condition of onset simultaneity). As P_i approaches infinity, A_i becomes approximately a unique or nonrecurring event.

"Regularity" of recurrence of events of class $A = R_a = (f)$ variance of P. (The size of variance of P is an index of the irregularity of the recurrence of events of the class A.)

"Interval" between recurring events of class $A = I = A_{j_{ON}} - A_{i_{OFF}}$:

$$\text{"Gap" or "Latency"} = I > 0;$$
$$\text{"Overlap"} = I < 0;$$
$$\text{"Continuity"} = I = 0.$$

"Order" relation for events A_i and $B_i = O_{ab} = A_{i_{ON}} - B_{i_{ON}} < 0 < B_{i_{ON}} - A_{i_{ON}}$. O_{ab} implies $B_i \not\rightarrow A_i$ (that is, if A precedes B, then B does not lead to A).

We propose that all other temporal parameters can be derived from these. Some examples are discussed below.

A "Rate" is a frequency of events of class A within a given time interval T_x, where $T_x = t_x - t_1$. A rate does not take into account the regularity of recurrence, nor the duration of each occurrence, except that some minimum duration is often used as a threshold value. An alternative for a threshold value is a minimum quantity or magnitude or amplitude of the event. But since magnitude has nothing to do with time, the present schema does not take magnitude into account at all. Events are defined as having only two states: ON and OFF. So there are no variations in magnitude, although some minimum detectable threshold level for an event to be observable (i.e., ON) is implicit in the system of definitions.

A "rhythm" is a pattern of periodicities, a *recurrent sequence of P values*. A "cycle" is the same thing as a period, namely: the time from one onset to the next onset for events of a given class. The term "cycle" usually is used with the implication that there are many recurrences and there is high regularity (low R) among them. An "oscillation," here, would be an *occurrence*, an OFF–ON–OFF sequence; but the term is more often used to imply a *recurrence*, or an ON–OFF–ON–OFF– ON . . . cycle. (When describing cycles and oscillations, one often makes reference to the amplitude and the mean level of the cycle. These terms refer to estimates of the magnitude of the events being measured, however, and so they are not *temporal* parameters, per se.)

There are several kinds of simultaneity. We have already noted "onset simultaneity." That is when you and I both start an activity, A, at the same time, although we may continue it for different lengths of time. Races are run with onset simultaneity (it is hoped) and with nonsimultaneity at the end (it is hoped). For this kind of simultaneity, $A_{i_{ON}}$ approximately equals $A_{j_{ON}}$, or the interval, $A_{j_{ON}}$ to $A_{i_{ON}}$, approaches zero. "Offset simultaneity" is a similar idea, meaning that we both cease a certain activity at the same time although we may have been engaging in it for different lengths of time. Offset simultaneity would occur if two people left a building together. For this kind of simultaneity, the interval $A_{j_{OFF}}$ to $A_{i_{OFF}}$ approaches zero.

This example reveals how arbitrary the definitions of ON and OFF states are. An OFF state with respect to an event defined in one certain way may just as well be regarded as an ON state with respect to a different construal of the event. Leaving a building is an OFF state with respect to being in or doing something in that building; but it is an ON state with respect to going somewhere else or doing something outside of that building. Which is the ON state, and indeed, what is the nature of the event, is of course a matter of definition and quite arbitrary.

We will define "strict simultaneity" as meaning that we both begin an activity at the same time ($A_{i_{ON}}$ to $A_{j_{ON}}$ approaches 0) *and* we both end it at the same time ($A_{i_{OFF}}$ to $A_{j_{OFF}}$ approaches 0). Strict simultaneity means we do the activity in *synchronization* (at least in regard to start and stop) as when two people sing a duet (it is to be hoped!). So, we could use "synchrony" as a synonym for strict simultaneity.

The term "synchronize," however, also means something else. While "synchronize" means to do two things at the same time, it also means to do two (or more) things in effective *coordination* with one another. "Coordinate" can mean doing the two things at different times, perhaps even at exactly out-of-phase times. Picture a pair of circus workers driving a tent stake together in a well-coordinated fashion. First, A strikes the stake with his or her sledgehammer while B raises his or her sledge, then B strikes while A winds up, and so forth. They are in perfect synchrony, but doing the focal activity (striking the stake with sledgehammers) at systematically different times. To avoid confusion of the term "synchrony," we will use "coordination," or "temporal coordination," for the case of the circus workers and the tent pole, and reserve "synchronization" for the case of the duet.

As is often the case, examples confound as well as clarify. Everyone will recognize that people singing a duet often sing in a coordinated fashion that is an out-of-synchrony pattern, much like the circus workers or often in an even more complex pattern. It is only the beginning and ending of their song, not the internal temporal structure of their singing, that is in synchrony in the strict simultaneity sense. So, perhaps, synchrony should be exemplified by a simpler action such as two people walking through a gate side by side. But even here, the idea of synchrony or strict simultaneity begins to slip away if we examine the arm, leg, and body movements of those two people at more and more micro levels.

Let us carry this argument several steps further. Whether or not $A_{j_{ON}}$ to $A_{i_{ON}}$ approaches zero closely enough to be considered simultaneous depends on the size of the unit time interval with which you are dealing. And that is defined as being of arbitrarily small size. If you have two simultaneous events (in any of the kinds of simultaneity) and you scale down the size of your minimum unit (say, from seconds to tenths of a second to milliseconds), you will eventually reach a scale at which the events are no longer simultaneous. Conversely, if you have two successive but nonsimultaneous events, and you scale up the size of your minimum unit (say, from seconds to minutes to hours) you will eventually reach a scale at which the events are simultaneous. So: *Simultaneity and succession, and hence, synchronization, coordination, duration, and rate, and therefore*

*periodicity, regularity, rhythm, and even order relations are all relative
to the arbitrary unit of measurement chosen for use.*

SOME KEY RESEARCH AREAS
FOR A SOCIAL PSYCHOLOGY OF TIME

We would like to end this book with a brief description of
some of the research areas that seem to us especially crucial
at this point in the development of a social psychology of time.
Some of these areas expand upon past research that has been
discussed earlier in this book, while some of them involve
temporal issues raised in the book for which there as yet has
been little research. Some are areas of study that we have not
reviewed here at all, but that would need further exploration
if we are to have a full-fledged social psychology of time. And
some of those areas would break new ground by bringing some
entirely new ideas into social psychology.

SOCIAL COGNITION AND THE JUDGMENT OF TIME

One area that we think ripe for advance is in the application
of recent models of social cognition (e.g., Wyer & Srull, 1980),
and of circadian processes (e.g., Moore-Ede *et al.*, 1982) to the
study of judgments of the passage of time. We think that those
models can provide the conceptual leverage needed to clear
up the long-standing puzzles within the psychophysics of time
(see Chapter 3; also see Doob, 1971; Ornstein, 1969). In our
treatment of that topic in Chapter 3, we proffered a formulation
involving assumptions both about information processing and
about the operation of physiological or psychological clocks.
Recent social cognition models of information processing, which
include ideas about priming, time delays, and the effects of
mood and other affective processes, seem ideally suited to
apply to the many mysteries in the research literature on the
experience of time. In Chapter 4, we discussed some of the

findings about physiological mechanisms underlying the entrainment of circadian rhythms. These can also be regarded as rudimentary forms of "biological clocks," and the work on human judgments of the passage of time might profit from the study of those circadian mechanisms. If those two sets of models are thoughtfully applied to modify our formulation (see Chapter 3), perhaps we can clear up some of the intriguing questions that have troubled scholars at least since William James.

SOCIAL ENTRAINMENT AND HUMAN INTERACTION

One of the most fruitful areas for research on temporal factors, we believe, is the study of entrainment and other temporal patterns in ongoing interpersonal interaction. Our own and other researchers' work on these questions, some of which is discussed in Chapter 4, point to the pervasiveness of cyclic processes in human interaction. That work shows temporal patterning in speech and silences, and in both the verbal and the nonverbal content of interaction. Collectively, the findings are quite complex. We think most of them can be accounted for within our social entrainment model (see Chapter 4). But whether that model or some other one is the most useful, we certainly need to bring such conceptual models to bear on future studies of entrainment and other temporal patterns. Furthermore, the study of social entrainment can profit from ideas already developed within biological science areas dealing with entrainment of circadian and other rhythms. Unfortunately, some of the work that arises out of the study of circadian rhythms from a biological science perspective (e.g., some of the research reviewed in Moore-Ede *et al.*, 1982; and in Luce, 1971) seems naive from a social psychological perspective. Conversely, some of the work on conversations that has been done from social-psychological or speech-communication perspectives seems naive from a biological perspective (e.g., some of the work on conversational synchrony reported in Argyle & Kendon, 1967). Our knowledge in this area will probably be advanced much more effectively by studies that blend ideas from both of the two disciplinary areas. Such integrative work, rare to date, is exemplified well in Warner's work on entrainment in conversations (Warner, 1979, 1984; Warner *et al.*, 1979).

SOCIAL ENTRAINMENT AND TASK PERFORMANCE

Another area we think profitable for advancing our knowledge about time is the study of how time pressure brings about social entrainment effects and modifies other temporal patterns in the task performance of individuals and groups. The work of our program described in Chapter 4 opens up this problem area. This research raises a number of interesting questions and suggests several avenues of attack. One promising approach would be to explore how entrainment effects vary as a function of differences in time pressure as compared to differences brought about by other ways of increasing task difficulty (e.g., by increases in total load or increases in item complexity). Another potential approach would be to explore the quantity–quality trade-offs in task performance, and how those are modified by various features of the task (e.g., task type, task load, task difficulty, time pressure), as well as by a variety of individual and group characteristics (e.g., specific aspects of individual abilities, motivations, and so on; group size, various aspects of group composition and structure; and the like). It also would be profitable and efficient, we believe, if such work on temporal patterns of task performance were tied into research on temporal patterns of interaction.

TEMPORAL FACTORS IN ROLE-BASED STRESS

The work we describe in Chapter 5 on time-based role stress is largely analytical, not empirical; and the work we describe in that same chapter on effects of shift work is largely based on a review of the research literature on that topic. Another very promising area for empirical research on temporal factors, therefore, is the study of time-based features of stress in work and nonwork roles. That research can probably best be done directly with respondents who already inhabit appropriate organizational settings; but if so, the research must take account of the complexities and constraints on research done in such natural settings. In any case, a key feature of that research might well be the description of ways in which individuals within complex work-role networks react to and cope with demands upon their time, as a function of features of their work group and situation, and as a function of features of their surrounding social networks (i.e., families, friends, nonwork organizations, etc.) We really have very little empirical information about *temporal* features of roles and stress and coping strategies. So we have much to gain from a systematic empirical exploration of temporal factors that influence the forms and levels of stress that people experience, and the various means they use for coping with such stress in work and nonwork roles. We also need a similar exploration of how temporal features of stress and coping strategies interact between work roles and nonwork roles. Furthermore, such work should try to examine entrainment effects from work schedules for "normal" work shifts as well as for off-time shifts. Finally, such work should explore further some of the concepts laid out in Chapter 5 that deal with the relation between temporal intervals and subsets of events: *versatility, flexibility, elasticity,* and *aggregatability.* Such work should not try to deal with the time–activity mapping in units so large as whole work shifts, or a night's sleep, but rather in smaller units such as "getting to work on Monday morning," "doing the week's laundry," and "my three o'clock meeting with a client." It is such midrange time units, rather than units either much smaller (the seconds and milliseconds of the psychophysics of time) or much larger, that most clearly violate the linear, homogeneous, absolute assumptions of Newtonian mathematical time. And it is from study of temporal patterns at the level of these temporal units that we are most likely to move toward an understanding of time at the social-psychological level.

FINAL COMMENT

We hope that readers will find this book provocative. We also hope they will be stimulated to consider study of temporal features in their own areas of research. We have tried to outline some tools in this final chapter: substantive, conceptual, and methodological ideas; some terms for a common language of time; and some research ideas. We encourage others to join with us in trying to define and develop a new area of social-psychological study, the social psychology of time.

REFERENCES

Allport, G. W., & Vernon, P. F. (1933). *Studies in expressive movement*. New York: Macmillan.

Altman, I. (1975). *The environment and social behavior: Privacy, personal space, territoriality and crossing*. Monterey, CA: Brooks-Cole.

Altman, I., & Taylor, D. A. (1973). *Social penetration: The development of interpersonal relationships*. New York: Holt, Rinehart & Winston.

Altman, I., Vinsel, A.M., & Brown, B.B. (1981). Dialectic conceptions in social psychology: An application to social penetration and privacy regulation. In L. Berkowitz (Ed.), *Advances in experimental social psychology* (Vol. 14, pp. 108–161). New York: Academic Press.

Argyle, M., & Dean, J. (1965). Eye contact, distance, and affiliation. *Sociometry, 28* 289–304.

Argyle, M., & Kendon, A. (1967). The experimental analysis of social performances In L. Berkowitz (Ed.), *Advances in experimental social psychology* (Vol. 3, pp. 55–99). New York: Academic Press.

Aschoff, J. (1981). Circadian rhythms: Interference with and dependence on work–rest schedules. In L.C. Johnson, D.I. Tepas, W. P. Colquhoun, & M. J. Colligan (Eds.), *The twenty-four hour workday: Proceedings of a symposium on variations in work–sleep schedules* (pp. 13–50). Cincinnati, OH: U.S. Department of Health and Human Services.

Asimov, I. (1968). *Of time and space and other things*. New York: Lancer Books.

Augustine, St. (1912). *St. Augustine's Confessions, Book 11*, Chapter 14 (W. Watts, Trans). Cambridge: Harvard University Press. (Quotation and citation extracted from Gorman, B. S., & Wessman, A. E. [1977]. Images, values and concepts of time in psychological research. In B. S. Gorman & A. E. Wessman (Eds.), *The personal experience of time* [pp. 218–219]. New York: Plenum.)

Bales, R. F. (1950). *Interaction process analysis: A method for the study of small groups*. Cambridge: Addison-Wesley.

Banks, O. (1956). Continuous shift work: The attitude of wives. *Industrial Psychology, 30*, 69–84.

Bell, C. R. (1965). Time estimation and increases in body temperature. *Journal of Experimental Psychology, 70*, 232–234.

Blakelock, E. (1960). A new look at the new leisure. *Administrative Science Quarterly, 4*, 446–467.

Campbell, D. T., & Stanley, J. C. (1966). *Experimental and quasi-experimental designs for research*. Chicago: Rand-McNally.

Capra, F. (1975). *The Tao of physics*. Berkeley: Shambhala.

Chapple, E. D. (1970). *Culture and biological man: Explorations in behavioral anthropology*. New York: Holt, Rinehart & Winston.

Cobb, L. (1973). *Time series analysis of the periodicities of casual conversations*. Unpublished doctoral dissertation, Cornell University.

Cohen, J. (1964). Psychological time. *Scientific American, 211* (5), 116–124.

Cohen, J. (1966). Subjective time. In J. T. Fraser (Ed.), *The voices of time* (pp. 257–275). New York: Braziller.

Colquhoun, W. P., Blake, M. J. F., & Edwards, R. S. (1968a). Experimental studies of shift work I: A comparison of "rotating" and "stabilized" 4-hour shift systems. *Ergonomics, 11*, 437–453.

Colquhoun, W. P., Blake, M. J. F., & Edwards, R. S. (1968b). Experimental studies of shift work II: Stabilized 8-hour shift systems. *Ergonomics, 11*, 527–546.

Colquhoun, W. P., Blake, M. J. F., & Edwards, R. S. (1969). Experimental studies of shift work III: Stabilized 12-hour shift systems. *Ergonomics, 12*, 865–882.

Cook, T. D., & Campbell, D. T. (1979). *Design and analysis of quasi-experiments for field settings*. Chicago: Rand-McNally.

Cottle, T. J. (1967). The circles test: An investigation of temporal relatedness and dominance. *Journal of Projective Techniques and Personality Assessment, 31*, 58–71.

Dabbs, J. (1983). *Fourier analysis and the rhythm of conversation* (Educational Research Information Clearinghouse (ERIC) Document ED 222 959).

deGrazia, S. (1972). Time and work. In H. Yaker, H. Osmond, & F. Cheek (Eds.), *The future of time* (pp. 439–479). New York: Anchor Books.

DeLaMare, G., & Walker, J. (1968). Factors influencing the choice of shift rotation. *Occupational Psychology, 42*, 1–21.

Doob, L. W. (1971). *Patterning of time*. New Haven: Yale University Press.

Dubin, R. (1973). Work and nonwork: Institutional perspectives. In M. D. Dunnette (Ed.), *Work and nonwork in the year 2001* (pp. 53–68). Monterey, CA: Brooks-Cole.

Fischer, R. (1966). Biological time. In J.T. Fraser (Ed), *The voices of time* (pp. 357–382). New York: Braziller.

Fraisse, P. (1963). *The psychology of time*. New York: Harper & Row.

Fraisse, P. (1984). Perceptions and estimation of time. *Annual Review of Psychology, 35*, 1–36.

Frankenhauser, M. (1959). *Estimation of time: An experimental study*. Stockholm: Almqvist & Wiksell.

Gergen, K. (1973). Social psychology as history. *Journal of Personality and Social Psychology, 26*, 309–320.

Gonzalez, A., & Zimbardo, P. G. (1985, March 3). Time in perspective. *Psychology Today*, pp. 20–26.

Goodwin, B. (1970). Biological stability. In C. H. Waddington (Ed.), *Toward a theoretical biology* (Vol 3, pp. 1–17). Chicago: Aldine.

Gordon, G. C., McGill, W. L., & Maltese, J. W. (1981). Home and community life of a sample of shift workers. In L. C. Johnson, D. I. Tepas, W. P. Colquhoun, & M. J. Colligan (Eds.), *The twenty-four hour workday: Proceedings of a symposium on variations in work–sleep schedules* (pp. 435–450). Cincinnati: U.S. Department of Health and Human Services.

Gottman, J.M. (1979). *Marital interaction: Experimental investigations*. New York: Academic Press.

Graham, R. J. (1981). The role perception of time in consumer research. *Journal of Consumer Research, 7,* 335–342.

Hackman, J. R. (1968). Effects of task characteristics on group products. *Journal of Experimental Social Psychology, 4,* 162–187.

Hamner, K. C. (1966). Experimental evidence for the biological clock. In J. T. Fraser (Ed.), *The voices of time* (pp. 281–295). New York: Braziller.

Hayes, D. P., & Cobb, L. (1979). Ultradian biorhythms in social interaction. In A. W. Siegman & S. Feldstein (Eds.), *Of speech and time: Temporal speech rhythms in interpersonal contexts* (pp. 57–80). Hillsdale, NJ: Erlbaum.

Heath, L. R. (1956). *The concept of time.* Chicago: The University of Chicago Press.

Hoagland, H. (1935). *Pacemakers in relation to aspects of behavior.* New York: Macmillan.

Iberall, A. S., & McCulloch, W. S. (1969). The organizing principle of complex living systems. *Journal of Basic Engineering, 91,* 290–294.

Jaffe, J., & Feldstein, S. (1970). *Rhythms of dialogue.* New York: Academic Press.

Johnson, L. C., Tepas, D. I., Colquhoun, W. P. & Colligan, M. J. (Eds.). (1981). *The twenty-four hour workday: Proceedings of a symposium on variations in work–sleep schedules.* Cincinnati: U.S. Department of Health and Human Services.

Jones, J. M. (1980). Conceptual and strategic issues in the relationship of black psychology to American social science. In A. W. Boykin, A. J. Franklin, & J. F. Yates (Eds), *Research directions of black psychologists* (pp. 390–432). New York: Russell Sage Foundation/Basic Books.

Kahn, R. L., Wolfe, D. M., Quinn, R. P., Snoek, J. D., & Rosenthal, R. A. (1964). *Organizational stress: Studies in role conflict and ambiguity.* New York: John Wiley & Sons.

Katz, D., & Kahn, R.L. (1976). *The social psychology of organizations* (2nd. ed.). New York: John Wiley & Sons.

Kelley, H. H., & Thibaut, J. W. (1978). *Interpersonal relations: A theory of interdependence.* New York: John Wiley & Sons.

Kelly, J. R. (1984). *Time limit and task type effects on individual and group performance and interaction.* Unpublished master's thesis, University of Illinois, Urbana.

Kelly, J. R., & McGrath, J. E. (1983). *Task load, time limits and production rates: Does work expand to fill the time available?.* (The Social Psychology of Time Research Program Report SPOT 83-1). Urbana: University of Illinois, Psychology Department.

Kelly, J. R., & McGrath, J. E. (1985). Effects of time limits and task types on task performance and interaction of four-person groups. *Journal of Personality and Social Psychology, 49,* 395–407.

Kendon, A. (1967). Some functions of gaze direction in social interaction. *Acta Psychologica, 26,* 1–47.

Klein, R., & Armitage, R. (1979). Rhythms in human performance: 1 1/2 hour oscillations in cognitive style. *Science, 204,* 1326–1328.

Kluckhohn, F. R., & Strodtbeck, F. L. (1961). *Variations in value orientations.* Evanston, IL: Row, Peterson.

Kulka, R. A. (1982). Monitoring social change via survey replication: Prospects and pitfalls from a replication survey of social roles and mental health. *Journal of Social Issues, 38*(4), 17–38.

Lakoff, G., & Johnson, M. (1980). *Metaphors we live by.* Chicago: University of Chicago Press.

Lass, N. J., & Lutz, D. R. (1975). The consistency of temporal speech characteristics in a repetitive oral reading task. *Language and Speech, 18,* 227–235.

Levine, R. V., & Bartlett, K. (1984). Pace of life, punctuality, and coronary heart disease in six countries. *Journal of Cross-Cultural Psychology, 15,* 2, 233–255.

Levine, R. V., West, L.J., & Reis, H. T. (1980). Perceptions of time and punctuality in the United States and Brazil. *Journal of Personality and Social Psychology, 38,* 4, 541–550.

Levine, R. V., & Wolff, E. (1985, March 3). Social time: The heartbeat of culture. *Psychology Today,* pp. 28–35.

Luce, G. (1971). *Biological rhythms in human and animal physiology.* New York: Dover.

Machatka, D. E. (1983). *Shiftwork and social perception of time* (The Social Psychology of Time Research Program Report SPOT 83-2). Urbana: University of Illinois, Psychology Department.

Maric, D. (1977). *Adapting working hours to modern needs.* Geneva: International Labour Office.

Maurice, M. (1975). *Shift work.* Geneva: International Labour Office.

McGrath, J. E. (Ed.). (1970). *Social and psychological factors in stress.* New York: Holt, Rinehart & Winston.

McGrath, J. E. (1964). *Groups: Interaction and performance.* Englewood, NJ: Prentice-Hall.

McGrath, J. E., Kelly, J. R., & Machatka, D. E. (1984). The social psychology of time: Entrainment of behavior in social and organizational settings. In S. Oskamp (Ed.), *Applied social psychology annual* (Vol. 5, pp. 21–44) Beverly Hills: Sage Publication.

McGrath, J. E., Martin, J., & Kulka, R. A. (1982). *Judgment calls in research.* Beverly Hills: Sage Publications.

McGrath, J.E., & Rotchford, N. L. (1983). Time and behavior in organizations. In L. Cummings & B. Staw (Eds.), *Research in Organizational Behavior* (Vol. 5, pp. 57–101). Greenwich, CT: JAI Press.

Melbin, M. (1978). Night as frontier. *American Sociological Review, 43,* 3–21.

Moore, W. E. (1963). *Man, time and society.* New York: John Wiley & Sons.

Moore-Ede, M. C., Sulzman, F. M., & Fuller, C. A. (1982). *The clocks that time us.* Cambridge, MA: Harvard University Press.

Mott, F. L. (1978). *Women, work, and family: Dimensions of change in American Society.* Lexington, MA: D. C. Heath.

Mott, F. L., Mann, F. C., McLoughlin, D., & Warwick, P. (1965). *Shift work: The social, psychological and physical consequences.* Ann Arbor: University of Michigan Press.

Nord, W. R., & Costigan, R. (1973). Worker adjustment to the four-day week: A longitudinal study. *Journal of Applied Psychology, 58,* 60–66.

Ornstein, R. E. (1969). *On the experience of time.* Middlesex, England: Penguin Books.

Parkinson, C. N. (1957). *Parkinson's Law.* Cambridge, MA: Riverdale Press.

Pittendrigh, C. S. (1972). On temporal organization in living systems. In H. Yaker, H. Osmond, & F. Cheek (Eds.), *The future of time* (pp. 179–218). New York: Anchor Books.

Prigogine, I. C., & Stengers, I. (1984). *Order out of chaos: Man's new dialogue with nature.* New York: Bantam Books.

Reinberg, A., Andlauer, P., & Vieux, N. (1981). Circadian temperature rhythm amplitude and long-term tolerance of shiftworking. In L. C. Johnson, D. I. Tepas, W. P. Colquhoun, & M.J. Colligan (Eds), *The twenty-four hour workday: Proceedings of a symposium on variations in work–sleep schedules* (pp. 87–104). Cincinnati: U. S. Department of Health and Human Services.

Robinson, J. P., & Converse, P. E. (1972). Social changes reflected in the use of time.

In A. Campbell & P. E. Converse (Eds.), *The human meaning of social change*. New York: Russell Sage Foundation.

Runkel, P. J., & McGrath, J. E. (1972). *Research on human behavior: A systematic guide to method*. New York: Holt, Rinehart & Winston.

Schachter, S., & Gross, L. P. (1968). Manipulated time and eating behavior. *Journal of Personality and Social Psychology, 10*, 98–106.

Sergean, R. (1971). *Managing shiftwork*. London: Gower Press.

Smoll, F. L. (1975). Between days consistency in personal tempo. *Perceptual and Motor Skills. 41*, 731–734.

Steiner, I. D. (1972). *Group process and productivity*. New York: Academic Press.

Strauss, A. (Ed.). (1965). *On social psychology by G. H. Mead*. Chicago: University of Chicago Press.

Takala, M. (1975). Consistency of psychomotor styles in interpersonal tempo. *Scandinavian Journal of Psychology, 16*, 193–202.

Tasto, D.L., Colligan, M. J., Skjei, E. W., & Polly, S. J (1978). *Health consequences of shift work*. Cincinnati: U.S. Department of Health of and Human Services.

Thibaut, J.W., & Kelley, H.H. (1959). *The social psychology of groups*. New York: John Wiley & Sons.

Walker, J. (1978). *The human aspects of shiftwork*. London: Institute of Personnel Management.

Warner, R. M. (1979). Periodic rhythms in conversational speech. *Language and speech, 22*, 381–396.

Warner, R. M. (1984). *Rhythm as an organizing principle in social interactions: Evidence of cycles in behavior and physiology*. Unpublished manuscript. Dover, NH.

Warner, R. M., Kenny, D. A., & Stoto, M. (1979). A new round robin analysis of variance for social interaction data. *Journal of Personality and Social Psychology, 37*, 1742–1757.

Webb, E J., Campbell, D. T., Schwartz, R. D., Sechrest, L., & Grove, J. B. (1981). *Nonreactive measures in the social sciences*. (2nd. ed.). Boston: Houghton Mifflin.

Wever, R. A. (1981). On varying work–sleep schedules: The biological rhythm perspective. In L. C. Johnson, D. I. Tepas, W. P. Colquhoun, & M. J. Colligan, (Eds). *The twenty-four hour work-day: Proceedings of a symposium on variations in work–sleep schedules* (pp. 51–86). Cincinnati: U. S. Department of Health and Human Services.

Wicker, A. W. (1979) *An introduction to ecological psychology*. Monterey, CA: Brooks-Cole.

Wyer, R. S. Jr., & Srull, T. K. (1980). The processing of social stimulus information: A conceptual integration. In R. Hastie, T. M. Ostrom, E B. Ebbesen, R. S. Wyer, Jr., D. L. Hamilton & D. E. Carlston (Eds.), *Person memory: The cognitive basis of social perception* (pp. 227–300). Hillsdale, NJ: Erlbaum.

I N D E X

Robinson, J. P., 66, 121, 178n.
Rosenthal, R. A., 6, 177n.
Rotchford, N. L., 47, 61, 62, 108, 178n.
Runkel, P. J., 68, 69, 131, 132, 135, 138, 179n.

Schachter, S., 78, 179n.
Schwartz, R. D., 158, 179n.
Sechrest, L., 158, 179n.
Sergean, R., 121, 179n.
Shift work, 117–125
Skjei, E. W., 121, 179n.
Smoll, F. L., 88, 179n.
Snoek, J. D., 6, 177n.
Srull, T. K., 170, 179n.
Stanley, J. C., 137, 138, 140, 144, 176n.
Steiner, I. D., 98, 179n.
Stengers, I., 29, 31, 32, 40, 178n.
Stoto, M., 88, 179n.
Strauss, A., 89, 179n.
Strodtbeck, F. L., 42, 64, 177n.
Sulzman, F. M., 47, 82, 178n.
Synchrony, 45–48, 89–103, 106–125

Takala, M., 88, 179n.
Task performance, 96–103
Tasto, D. L., 121, 179n.
Taylor, D. A., 5, 6, 92, 175n.
TEMPO (see Entrainment, Social entrainment model)
Temponomics, 61–64
Temporal issues, 12, 13, 107–117
    individual, 111–114
    individual–organization interface, 114–117
    organization, 107–110
Temporal paradigms, 10, 26–49, 163, 164
    Classical (see Newtonian)
    Eastern mysticism, 26–36
    Einsteinian (see New Physics)
    Newtonian, 26–36, 52–61, 67

New Physics, 26–36, 40, 41, 62
    Transactional, 27–36, 54–61, 67
Temporal orientations, 61–67
Temporal parameters, 165–170
Tepas, D. I., 120, 177n.
Thibaut, J. W., 5, 6, 113, 177n., 179n.
Time
    cultural differences in, 10, 11, 52–67
    flow of, 25, 26, 28–31
    frames, 50–67
    judgments of, 11, 67–78, 170, 171
    philosophical issues in, 18–26
    psychological experience of, 11, 67–78
    psychophysics of, 11, 68–71
    reality of, 23–25, 28–31
    role-based stress, effects of time in, 6, 7, 12, 13, 105–117, 172, 173
    social cognition, 67–78, 170, 171
    social psychology, role of time in, 1–15, 165, 170–174
    structure of, 22, 23, 28–31
    validity of, 19–22, 28–31

Vernon, P. F., 88, 175n.
Vieux, N., 121, 178n.
Vinsel, A. M., 5, 92, 175n.

Walker, J., 120, 121, 176n., 179n.
Warner, R. M., 88–90, 93, 94, 172, 179n.
Warwick, P., 120, 121, 178n.
Webb, E. J., 158, 179n.
West, L. J., 65, 178n.
Wever, R. A., 121, 179n.
Wicker, A. W., 95, 114, 179n.
Wolfe, D. M., 6, 177n.
Wolfe, E., 65, 66, 178n.
Work, 12, 13, 105–125
Wyer, R. S., Jr., 170, 179n.

Zimbardo, P. G., 65, 66, 176n.